THE THIRTEEN COLONIES FROM FOUNDING TO REVOLUTION IN AMERICAN HISTORY

Pat McCarthy

Enslow Publishers, Inc.

40 Industrial Road   PO Box 38
Box 398   Aldershot
Berkeley Heights, NJ 07922 Hants GU12 6BP
USA   UK

http://www.enslow.com

Library of Congress Cataloging-in-Publication Data

McCarthy, Pat, 1940–
    The Thirteen Colonies from founding to revolution in American history/ Pat McCarthy.
        p. cm. —(In American history)
    Summary: Discusses each colony's history individually including its settlement, naming, laws, and prominent persons.
    Includes bibliographical references (p.) and index.
    ISBN 0-7660-1990-X
    1. United States—History—Colonial period, ca. 1600–1775—Juvenile literature. 2. United States—History—Revolution, 1775–1783—Juvenile literature. 3. United States—History—Confederation, 1783–1789—Juvenile literature. [1. United States—History—Colonial period, ca. 1600–1775. 2. United States—History—Revolution, 1775–1783.] I. Title. II. Series.
    E188.M116   2004
    973.2—dc22

                                                    2003016424

Printed in the United States of America

10 9 8 7 6 5 4 3 2 1

To Our Readers: We have done our best to make sure all Internet Addresses in this book were active and appropriate when we went to press. However, the author and the publisher have no control over and assume no liability for the material available on those Internet sites or on other Web sites they may link to. Any comments or suggestions can be sent by e-mail to comments@enslow.com or to the address on the back cover.

★ CONTENTS ★

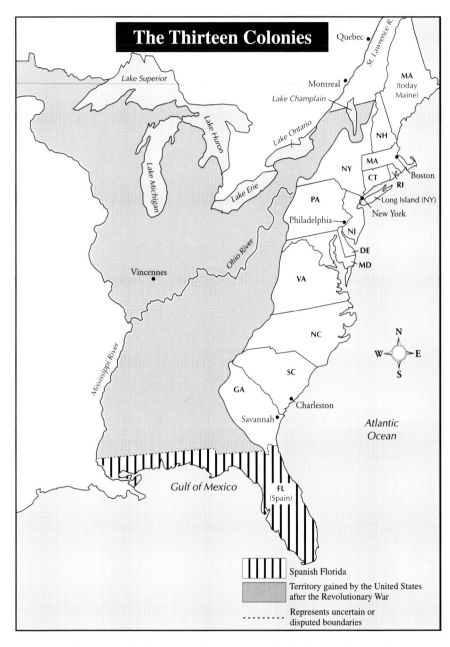

The Thirteen Colonies

Quebec

St. Lawrence R.

MA (today Maine)

Montreal

Lake Champlain

Lake Superior

Lake Huron

Lake Ontario

NH

Lake Michigan

Lake Erie

NY

MA

CT

Boston

RI

Long Island (NY)

New York

PA

Philadelphia

NJ

Ohio River

DE

MD

Vincennes

VA

N

NC

W E

S

SC

Mississippi River

GA

Charleston

Savannah

Atlantic Ocean

Gulf of Mexico

FL (Spain)

Spanish Florida

Territory gained by the United States after the Revolutionary War

Represents uncertain or disputed boundaries

The original thirteen colonies stretched down almost the entire eastern seaboard of the present-day United States.

The date was August 2, 1776. About fifty men gathered in the State House in Philadelphia. Among the men were two future presidents, three future vice presidents, and ten future members of Congress. The men included lawyers, merchants, farmers, plantation owners, doctors, ministers, and a surveyor.

THE COLONIES DECLARE INDEPENDENCE

They had gathered to sign the Declaration of Independence, asserting the freedom of the thirteen American colonies from England. They had approved the Declaration on July 4, after voting for independence two days earlier. By July 19, the document had been approved by all the colonies. Then, it had been handwritten in ornamental script on parchment with a quill pen. It was finally completed.

Signing the Document

John Hancock, president of the Second Continental Congress (a group of delegates from all the colonies), stepped up first. He signed in large, bold letters directly below the text in the center of the page. Most of the men signed by geographic location. The signatures at the top

WHEN IN THE COURSE OF HUMAN EVENTS, IT BECOMES NECESSARY FOR ONE PEOPLE TO DISSOLVE THE POLITICAL BANDS WHICH HAVE CONNECTED THEM WITH ANOTHER, AND TO ASSUME, AMONG THE POWERS OF THE EARTH, THE SEPARATE AND EQUAL STATION TO WHICH THE LAWS OF NATURE AND OF NATURE'S GOD ENTITLE THEM, A DECENT RESPECT TO THE OPINIONS OF MANKIND REQUIRES THAT THEY SHOULD DECLARE THE CAUSES WHICH IMPEL THEM TO THE SEPARATION.

WE HOLD THESE TRUTHS TO BE SELF-EVIDENT, THAT ALL MEN ARE CREATED EQUAL, THAT THEY ARE ENDOWED BY THEIR CREATOR WITH CERTAIN UNALIENABLE RIGHTS, THAT AMONG THESE ARE LIFE, LIBERTY, AND THE PURSUIT OF HAPPINESS. THAT TO SECURE THESE RIGHTS, GOVERNMENTS ARE INSTITUTED AMONG MEN, DERIVING THEIR JUST POWERS FROM THE CONSENT OF THE GOVERNED, THAT WHENEVER ANY FORM OF GOVERNMENT BECOMES DESTRUCTIVE OF THESE ENDS, IT IS THE RIGHT OF THE PEOPLE TO ALTER OR TO ABOLISH IT, AND TO INSTITUTE NEW GOVERNMENT, LAYING ITS FOUNDATION ON SUCH PRINCIPLES AND ORGANIZING ITS POWERS IN SUCH FORM, AS TO THEM SHALL SEEM MOST LIKELY TO EFFECT THEIR SAFETY AND HAPPINESS.[1]

In the Declaration of Independence, *Thomas Jefferson outlined what the American patriots felt were the basic rights of man.*

were those of the delegates from the northern colonies, and the delegates from Georgia, the southernmost state, signed last.[2]

Fifty-six men signed the Declaration of Independence. As these men were signing the declaration, the Continental Army was scrambling to get organized for the long fight ahead against the British. Colonists worried about the threat of British ships off the coast.

Coming Together as a Nation

The signers of the Declaration came from thirteen colonies, settled by people from many different European

In the early nineteenth century, John Trumbull painted this depiction of the signing of the Declaration of Independence. John Hancock is seated in the chair and standing to the left of him are (from left to right): John Adams, Roger Sherman, Robert R. Livingston, Thomas Jefferson, and Benjamin Franklin.

countries. However, the majority of the colonists was of British background. Several religions and political views were represented. How did these thirteen very different colonies come together as one to declare their independence from England?

As the colonies prospered and grew, the colonists had become more self-sufficient. As a result, they wanted more say in their government. For years, many of the colonies were almost self-governing, as England was so far away.

After 1763, England had realized how strong and self-sufficient the colonies had grown, and felt a need to assert its authority over them.

Colonists Resent British Taxes

The French and Indian War (1754–1763) and its counterpart in Europe, the Seven Years' War (1756–1763), had been expensive. England's Parliament felt that because the war in the colonies was fought to ensure the safety of the colonists, they should help pay for future protection.

England started imposing taxes on the colonies. First was the Sugar Act in 1764. The colonists were only mildly irritated by it. Next came the Stamp Act a year later. Colonists were upset over this tax, as they had to pay for stamps on all legal documents. Stamps were even required on newspapers, almanacs, and playing cards.

The colonists reacted by calling the Stamp Act Congress. Delegates from nine colonies met in New York City. They petitioned the king and Parliament. They stated their loyalty to the king, but made it clear that they believed the colonies could only be taxed through their own assemblies.

Colonists Take Action

Several riots occurred in connection with the Stamp Act. The Sons of Liberty, a radical organization, was started in Boston in 1765. The Stamp Act was repealed in 1766. The same day, Parliament passed the Declaratory Act, which said that Parliament had authority over the colonies in all things.

The colonists' pleasure at the repeal of the Stamp Act did not last long. In 1767, Parliament passed the Townshend Acts. Taxes were levied on many goods the colonies imported from England, such as lead, paint, paper, and tea.

The Massachusetts General Assembly contacted other colonial governments, urging them to protest the new taxes. Boston merchants organized another boycott of British goods, and the merchants of Philadelphia and New York City joined in a nonimportation agreement. Some of the southern colonies also joined in.

Problems in Boston with the British

England placed four regiments of troops in Boston. Bostonians resented their presence, and on March 5, 1770, the Boston Massacre occurred. Several young men threw rocks and snowballs at the British sentries. One of the soldiers was knocked down, and in the scuffle, several British soldiers fired into the crowd, killing five people.

The Townshend Acts had been repealed, but the news had not reached the colonies before this incident occurred.

In 1772, Samuel Adams suggested creation of "committees of correspondence" by which the colonies could keep in touch about their problems with England. John Dickinson, a Philadelphia lawyer, published a pamphlet called *Letters From a Farmer in Pennsylvania to the Inhabitants of the British Colonies*, which said that people should not be taxed without representation.

In 1773, the Tea Act was passed, taxing tea sent to the colonies. On December 16, the infamous Boston Tea Party occurred. Members of the Sons of Liberty, dressed as Mohawk Indians, boarded a ship and threw the tea into the harbor.

The First Continental Congress

The First Continental Congress met in Philadelphia in 1774 to decide how to react to what they saw as unfair British actions. Delegates from all the colonies except Georgia were present. They sent a statement of grievances to the king. They also agreed to stop all trade with Great Britain, and to meet the following year.

On April 18, 1775, British soldiers tried to seize the gunpowder stored in Concord, Massachusetts. The local colonial soldiers, called minutemen, fought them, in the Battles of Lexington and Concord.

The next year, independence was declared. However, before these colonies officially broke ties with Britain, each of them had its own rich history.

In December 1606, three ships carrying 144 men left London. They had received a charter, or grant, from King James I for land located in North America. The Spanish had brought back gold from South America and the Caribbean, so the British

VIRGINIA

dreamed of the riches that they would find. Only 104 settlers survived the stormy voyage.[1]

Choosing a Site

After four months at sea, Captain Christopher Newport's crew sighted land on April 26, 1607. They spent two weeks exploring the Chesapeake Bay area, looking for a good site for their settlement. The site they chose was about twenty miles up a river. The colonists named the waterway the James River and the settlement Jamestown after their king.

Jamestown was located on a peninsula, a piece of land with water on three sides. This would make it easy to defend against possible American Indian attacks. The colonists ignored advice to avoid "a low and moist place because it will prove unhealthful."[2]

It was true. Enormous swarms of mosquitoes made life uncomfortable, and there was no fresh water for drinking. George Percy, a prominent settler, wrote that during the first year, "Our men were destroyed with cruell diseases . . . some departed suddenly, but for the most part they died of meere famine. There were never Englishmen left in a foreigne countrey in such miserie as wee were in this new discovered Virginia."[3]

Hard Times in Virginia

The settlers were gentlemen—they were not used to working. They searched for gold rather than planting crops. This was one reason they nearly starved that first winter. Only corn, bread, meat, and fish from the Algonquian Indians saved them.

More settlers arrived in late 1607 and 1608. Captain John Smith became the leader of Jamestown in 1608. He insisted all the men work, rather than hunt for gold. At one point, he was captured by American Indians.

Pocahontas

John Smith said that at the moment when he thought the American Indians would kill him, the chief's little daughter, Pocahontas, ran out and begged her father to spare him. After this, Smith was able to set up trade with Chief Powhatan's tribe. However, Smith was injured in a gunpowder explosion in October of 1609 and had to return to England.

The winter of 1609–1610 was known as the "starving time." One survivor wrote of the regret that many colonists felt over the loss of Smith before that winter,

James Fort was built during the time that John Smith was an influential leader in the colony at Jamestown, Virginia.

"Now we all found the losse of Captaine *Smith*, yea his greatest maligners could now curse his losse."[4]

Things Slowly Get Better

The first women arrived in Jamestown in 1611. They brought livestock and food supplies, as well. These factors helped the colony to stabilize.

Late that year, some of the settlers moved from Jamestown to a small island upriver, where they started the town of Henrico. That same year, plots of land were assigned to men for their own use. Prior to this, all land had been owned in common, and all food went into a common store, to be distributed to everyone.

Tobacco Is Introduced

In 1612, John Rolfe introduced tobacco to Virginia. He planted seed from the West Indies. Within the next two years, he was exporting tobacco to England. It became Virginia's most important crop.

By 1616, 1,650 settlers had come to Virginia, and 1,000 of them had died. Three hundred had returned to England. However, by 1619, the population of Virginia had grown to over one thousand people.[5] That year, another 1,261 new settlers arrived in the colony, including families. The ninety young single women who arrived soon married settlers.

A group of representatives from various plantations of Virginia began meeting. This governing assembly became known as the House of Burgesses.

The First Africans Arrive in Virginia

Africans were brought to North America in 1619. Historians are unclear whether they were indentured servants or slaves; either way, they worked on tobacco plantations.

Indentured servants were brought from England in 1619. Under the system, a planter paid the laborer's passage to America. In exchange, the man worked four or five years for the planter with no pay, then he was free. He was provided room and board while he worked.

At first indentured servitude was the primary source of labor. After a couple of generations, however, slavery overtook indentured servitude as the main source of labor. Slaves were forced to work for no pay for their whole lives. Raising tobacco required a great deal of human labor. Planters could profit more if they did not have to pay workers, so slavery spread quickly.

The headright system also began in the early seventeenth century. Any Englishman who paid for his family's passage to America received fifty acres for each person he brought to the New World.

Troubles With American Indians Begin

Until 1622, there had been few problems with the American Indians. But Powhatan, the friendly Algonquian ruler, died, and his brother, Opechancanough, took over. The American Indians grew more concerned about the settlers seizing their land. On March 22, they launched an organized series of attacks along the James River.

They killed over three hundred fifty settlers and burned their property.

The settlers retaliated, killing many American Indians and destroying their villages and crops. The American Indians were forced to withdraw.

Virginia Becomes a Crown Colony

In 1624, Virginia became a Crown Colony, under royal rule. Although its powers were weakened, the General Assembly continued to meet irregularly. County courts were set up and clerks, sheriffs, justices of the peace, coroners, and constables were named.

There were a few large plantations, but most Virginians had small farms. They grew food for themselves and tobacco to sell.

In 1639, the House of Burgesses and the Governor's Council were approved by the king. These two bodies now made up the General Assembly, which governed Virginia.

The Church of England was the official church of the colony. The church was the center of worship and social activities. It kept the records of christenings, marriages, and deaths.

Berkley as Governor

In 1642, Sir William Berkeley became governor of Virginia. He was quite popular. During his term, there was a steady stream of settlers. In England, the oldest son inherited all the land; many younger sons emigrated to America so they could own land.

The English Civil War (1642–1649) was underway. Virginia and Berkeley were loyal to King Charles I when the rebels forced the king into hiding and took over England. Many of those loyal to the king escaped and settled in Virginia.

More American Indian Problems

In 1644, the American Indians attacked all points along the frontier. Opechancanough was old and weak, but he was still behind the attacks. More than five hundred colonists died.

Berkeley's forces killed many American Indians, burned their villages, and destroyed their crops. They captured Opechancanough and brought him back to Jamestown. He was blind and could not walk. One of the Virginia soldiers, resenting Berkeley's respectful treatment of Opechancanough, shot the old chief in the back.

The next year, the General Assembly authorized the building of several frontier forts. They served as protection from the American Indians and as bases for explorers and traders going into the west of the main settlements in Virginia.

Tobacco Growers Are Unhappy

For fifteen years, Virginians prospered. Prices for tobacco were good. However, in 1660, the king was restored to the English throne. Charles II was not sympathetic to the colony. He and Parliament worked with London merchants to give most of the profit from tobacco to the merchants instead of the Virginia farmers. Colonists made little profit and were allowed to sell tobacco only to England.

The Backcountry v. the Tidewater Aristocracy

The settlements in the west, or the backcountry, were growing and becoming more prosperous. The settlers became unhappy about their lack of representation in the House of Burgesses. Some of the western settlements had more people than the eastern, or "tidewater," settlements, but each county had two representatives.

The "tidewater aristocracy," as the influential people in the east were called, had no sympathy for the "backcountry" settlers and their problems.

Bacon's Rebellion

In the 1670s, American Indian attacks increased, and Berkeley told the colonists not to retaliate. A group of settlers, under Nathaniel Bacon, decided to take matters into its own hands. Bacon and his men tried to seize land from the American Indians. A bloody battle ensued, and several hundred Virginians were killed.

Bacon insisted that the governor send the militia to wipe out the American Indians, but Berkeley ordered his men to just guard the settlements. They were not to attack the American Indians.

Berkeley called for a new election of members to the House of Burgesses, hoping to increase support for himself. Bacon was elected by a huge margin, and came with his army to Jamestown to take over his seat. Bacon's

Rebellion resulted in the burning of the capital and Berkeley being forced to flee. Bacon soon died of dysentery, and Berkeley regained control, executing many of Bacon's followers.

Virginia's Population Grows

Settlements had spread beyond the Fall Line (between the plains and the plateau), and American Indian attacks were fewer. Refugees called Huguenots came from France, where they were not allowed to practice their religion. Pioneers went up the James, Rappahannock, and Roanoke rivers. At the same time, Scotch-Irish and Germans from Pennsylvania, another English colony, settled in the Shenandoah Valley.

By the early 1750s, many Christian faiths were represented in Virginia, including Presbyterian, Lutheran, German Reformed, Mennonite, Baptist, and Quaker. The Church of England was still the state church, but others were allowed to practice their faiths.

During the early 1700s, Virginian plantation owners became more prosperous. Worked by slaves, the plantations grew and so did the production of tobacco. Many small farmers went out of business because they could not afford to pay laborers.

Virginia's Involvement in the French and Indian War

Robert Dinwiddie became governor in 1751. The French and the English both had been trying to settle the Ohio Valley. Dinwiddie sent George Washington in 1753 to inform the French in the Ohio Valley that they were on English land. The French ignored the message.

The next year, Washington and a small force defeated a group of French at Great Meadows, near the present juncture of Pennsylvania, West Virginia, and Virginia. Then, a large group of French and American Indians attacked his men.

Dinwiddie asked England for aid, and they sent General Edward Braddock with two regiments of men. Washington served as Braddock's aide. Braddock was killed in the battle for Fort Duquesne, which later became Pittsburgh. Washington escaped, and was made commander of the Virginia forces.

British Levy Taxes on the Colonists

As Virginia became more prosperous and self-sufficient, resentment against the British grew. When England implemented the Stamp Act in 1756, most Virginians opposed it. They also resented the Townshend Acts. Colonists believed that only their local legislatures had a right to tax

George Washington rose up to become the most prominent Virginian.

them. In late 1772, when the British blockaded Boston Harbor, Virginia sent food and money to help the people of Boston. Lord Dunmore, governor of Virginia, supported the British and dissolved the House of Burgesses.

Virginia Colonists React to British

The year of 1774 was a busy one. In July, George Washington and George Mason held a meeting at the Fairfax County Courthouse. From this meeting came the Fairfax Resolves, a list of the beliefs of the colonists. Among them was the belief that they should be free to make their own laws and levy their own taxes. They also called for a Congress of representatives from all the colonies, and appointed George Washington and George Gent as their representatives.

Lord Dunmore's War

Lord Dunmore's War against the American Indians also occurred in 1774. He sent one thousand men to the Little Kanawha River to attack the Shawnee. This was in present-day West Virginia. The Battle of Point Pleasant took place on October 10. Dunmore's forces drove the Shawnee leader, Cornstalk, and his followers north of the Ohio River. The Shawnee then signed a treaty that opened land east and south of the Ohio River for settlement.

Preparing for Independence

Virginia sent representatives to the First Continental Congress in Philadelphia in September 1774. The

SOURCE DOCUMENT

5. RESOLVED THAT THE CLAIM LATELY ASSUMED AND EXERCISED BY THE BRITISH PARLIAMENT, OF MAKING ALL SUCH LAWS AS THEY THINK FIT, TO GOVERN THE PEOPLE OF THESE COLONIES, AND TO EXTORT FROM US OUR MONEY WITH OUT OUR CONSENT, IS NOT ONLY DIAMETRICALLY CONTRARY TO THE FIRST PRINCIPLES OF THE CONSTITUTION, AND THE ORIGINAL COMPACTS BY WHICH WE ARE DEPENDANT UPON THE BRITISH CROWN AND GOVERNMENT; BUT IS TOTALLY INCOMPATIBLE WITH THE PRIVILEGES OF A FREE PEOPLE, AND THE NATURAL RIGHTS OF MANKIND; WILL RENDER OUR OWN LEGISLATURES MERELY NOMINAL AND NUGATORY, AND IS CALCULATED TO REDUCE US FROM A STATE OF FREEDOM AND HAPPINESS TO SLAVERY AND MISERY.[6]

Unhappy colonists expressed their discontent with the British government through the Fairfax Resolves.

delegates adopted a Declaration of Rights, which outlined the rights that they believed Parliament had violated.

On March 23, 1775, a Virginia convention meeting in Richmond voted to prepare the colony for defense, as they anticipated British action against the colonies. That action came on April 18, when British troops attacked the Minutemen at Lexington and Concord in Massachusetts. The colonies were at war. Patrick Henry summed up the thoughts of many with his famous statement, "I know not what course others may take, but as for me, give me liberty or give me death."[7]

MASSACHUSETTS

American Indians lived in Massachusetts for thousands of years before the white settlers arrived. During the three years before the first permanent colonists came, 90 percent of the Massachusetts Bay Indians were killed by diseases, including influenza and smallpox.[1] They got these diseases from English and Dutch fishermen, who visited the area. Because the Indians had never developed any immunity to the diseases, their population was nearly wiped out.

Arrival of the Pilgrims

The Pilgrims had left England because of persecution by the king. Many of the Pilgrims wanted nothing to do with the Church of England so they were called Separatists. They spent several years in Holland, then sailed for the New World with some other settlers who were not Separatists.

The Pilgrims arrived on December 26, 1620. Under Governor John Carver, they established the first permanent settlement in New England at Plymouth. Their plan of government was called the Mayflower Compact. It was named after the ship in which they sailed to the New World. The compact established a government for the Pilgrims and declared their loyalty to the king.

IN THE NAME OF GOD, AMEN. WE, WHOSE NAMES ARE UNDERWRITTEN, THE LOYAL SUBJECTS OF OUR DREAD SOVEREIGN LORD KING JAMES, BY THE GRACE OF GOD, OF GREAT BRITAIN, FRANCE, AND IRELAND, KING, DEFENDER OF THE FAITH, &C. HAVING UNDERTAKEN FOR THE GLORY OF GOD, AND ADVANCEMENT OF THE CHRISTIAN FAITH, AND THE HONOUR OF OUR KING AND COUNTRY, A VOYAGE TO PLANT THE FIRST COLONY IN THE NORTHERN PARTS OF VIRGINIA; DO BY THESE PRESENTS, SOLEMNLY AND MUTUALLY, IN THE PRESENCE OF GOD AND ONE ANOTHER, COVENANT AND COMBINE OURSELVES TOGETHER INTO A CIVIL BODY POLITICK, FOR OUR BETTER ORDERING AND PRESERVATION, AND FURTHERANCE OF THE ENDS AFORESAID: AND BY VIRTUE HEREOF DO ENACT, CONSTITUTE, AND FRAME, SUCH JUST AND EQUAL LAWS, ORDINANCES, ACTS, CONSTITUTIONS, AND OFFICERS, FROM TIME TO TIME, AS SHALL BE THOUGHT MOST MEET AND CONVENIENT FOR THE GENERAL GOOD OF THE COLONY; UNTO WHICH WE PROMISE ALL DUE SUBMISSION AND OBEDIENCE. IN WITNESS WHEREOF WE HAVE HEREUNTO SUBSCRIBED OUR NAMES AT CAPE-COD THE ELEVENTH OF NOVEMBER, IN THE REIGN OF OUR SOVEREIGN LORD KING JAMES, OF ENGLAND, FRANCE, AND IRELAND, THE EIGHTEENTH, AND OF SCOTLAND THE FIFTY-FOURTH, ANNO DOMINI; 1620.[2]

The Mayflower Compact was signed by forty-one of the Pilgrims onboard the ship the Mayflower, *after which the document was named.*

The Pilgrims Face Hardships

Although the Pilgrims endured many hardships, their settlement did not fail. The local American Indians, the Wampanoag, taught them to survive in the wilderness. An American Indian called Squanto and the chief, Massasoit, became their good friends. In 1621, the Pilgrims and the Wampanoag celebrated the first Thanksgiving.

Pilgrim Edward Winslow wrote:

Our harvest being gotten in . . . many of the Indians coming amongst us, and among the rest, their greatest king, Massasoit, with some 90 men, whom for three days we entertained and feasted; and they went out

American Indian leader Massasoit visited the Pilgrims and offered his help to the colonists.

and killed five deer, which they brought to the plantation . . .[3]

The Puritans Settle Massachusetts Bay

In 1628, another shipload of people arrived from England. Like the Separatists, they were also unhappy with the church. Because they only wanted to reform the Church of England, not separate from it, they called themselves Puritans. They settled in Salem. The next year, the king granted a royal charter to them for the Massachusetts Bay colony.

Another group of Puritans, led by John Winthrop, arrived in 1630 and settled in Charlestown, now part of Boston. By 1640, there were twenty thousand settlers in Massachusetts.[4] Settlement spread along the coast and westward.

Most settlers worked small farms. The towns had houses around a central square, and the fields were outside the towns. Each town held town meetings, where everyone had a say in governing the town.

Puritans Persecute People of Other Faiths

In spite of the persecution they had endured in England, the Puritans were not tolerant of others who wanted to worship in their own ways. Roger Williams, a young minister, preached that the land belonged to the American Indians, not to England or the Massachusetts Bay Colony.

William Bradford, a Puritan, wrote that Williams was "a man godly and zealous . . . but very unsettled in judgmente."[5] Williams was tried by the Massachusetts General Court and found guilty of spreading dangerous ideas. They ordered him out of the colony, and he fled to friendly American Indians in what is now Rhode Island.

Anne Hutchinson also challenged Puritan beliefs. She claimed that people could communicate directly with God and be assured they would go to heaven when they died. She developed a large following in Boston, and the Puritans recognized her as a threat. She was tried in 1638 and banished from the colony. She also went to what is now Rhode Island.

Few Quakers settled in the Massachusetts area because of religious persecution. Those who did soon moved to Rhode Island, where they were welcome.

American Indian Problems Begin

At first, relations with the American Indians were friendly. The exception was the Pequot Indians, who were also enemies of the Wampanoag. In 1636, a trader, John Oldham, was killed by Narrragansett Indians on Block Island. A military force of ninety men under John Endicott killed fourteen of the Block Islanders and burned their village and crops.

Angered, the Pequot attacked the village of Wethersfield, killing several people and capturing two young girls. On May 26, 1637, John Mason led a group from Connecticut in an attack on the Pequot village near New Haven. They wiped out almost the entire Pequot tribe.

King Philip's War

Things were again peaceful for a while. Then, Massasoit died in 1661. His son, Metacomet, became chief in 1662, after a brief reign by his older brother. Metacomet, called King Philip by the Europeans, resented the settlers and attacked them in 1675. Sixteen towns were wiped out. The conflict, called King Philip's War, ended in 1676 when King Philip was hunted down and killed.

Dominion of New England Formed

In 1684, the Massachusetts Bay charter was revoked. Massachusetts Bay became part of the royal colony of New England, set up by King James II. He fell from power and, in 1691, Massachusetts absorbed the Maine and Plymouth colonies and became a royal province. The colonists were not happy with the new charter, as it took away some of their liberties. This was the beginning of the discontent with England.

Witchcraft

In the 1680s and early 1690s, hysteria swept through the colony, as many were accused of being witches. In Salem, several hundred people were arrested and jailed. Nineteen of those accused were executed during the Salem witchcraft trials of 1692. Increase Mather, president of Harvard, said during the height of the hysteria in Salem, "I am abundantly satisfied that there have been, and are still most cursed Witches in the Land."[6]

Smallpox

Several smallpox outbreaks in the early 1700s killed many in the colony. By 1763, inoculation was helping to prevent deaths from the disease. A tiny amount of the live germ was injected under the skin of the person in order to make him or her immune to smallpox.

England Taxes the Colonists

In 1764, England passed the Sugar Act. It kept Massachusetts from trading with the West Indies, its biggest moneymaking source.

The Stamp Act of 1765 angered many Massachusetts colonists. They resented being taxed by Parliament when they had no representation. Massachusetts settler James Otis persuaded delegates from nine colonies to meet in New York in October 1765 as the "Stamp Act Congress." Citizens rioted in Boston, and many of the stamp agents resigned.

British Troops Arrive in Boston

In 1768, British troops were sent to Boston to control the colonists. On March 5, 1770, the Boston Massacre occurred. Afterward, the British commander, Thomas Preston, was put on trial. However, his lawyers, including John Adams, successfully defended him and he was found not guilty. Although most Bostonians were patriots, many Loyalists, who were loyal to England and the king, also lived there.

Colonists Take Steps to Remedy Problems With Britain

In 1772, Samuel Adams, a colonial leader in Boston, established committees of correspondence to keep communication open between Massachusetts towns. He encouraged other colonies to do the same. Soon, the colonies were also corresponding among one another.

Bostonians resented the tax levied on tea in 1773. On December 16, patriots dressed as American Indians boarded three ships in Boston Harbor and threw the tea overboard. Britain responded by closing Boston Harbor, reducing Massachusetts's power of self-government, and forcing citizens to quarter troops in their homes. Closing the harbor also hurt the colony financially.

The Boston Tea Party was an early rebellion against the British king. Colonists were trying to show Britian that they felt the tea tax was unfair.

Preparation for War

The colonists began training their militias, or local troops, for war. They gathered arms and ammunition and drilled in the village greens. The militias in Massachusetts called themselves minutemen, saying they were ready to fight "at a minute's notice."

On April 18, 1775, minuteman Paul Revere learned that the British planned to seize gunpowder stored in Concord. Revere, along with another minuteman named William Dawes, rode throughout the countryside, alerting the colonists.

The Revolutionary War Begins

The next day, a company of minutemen met British troops at Lexington. Eight minutemen were killed and ten were wounded. All along the road to Concord and on the way back to Boston, the British were attacked by Minutemen hiding behind trees and rocks. By the end of the day, the colonists had inflicted 273 casualties on the British.[7] The Revolutionary War had begun.

NEW HAMPSHIRE

When the first white people arrived, New Hampshire was populated by Algonquin Indians living in villages near fresh water. They lived by hunting and fishing, and made tools from stone.

In the year 1603, an Englishman, Captain Bartholomew Gosnold, was the first European to land on the New Hampshire Coast. He was followed by Martin Pring later that year, and Samuel de Champlain in 1605.

Captain John Smith of Virginia was sent by the king in 1614 to map the area. He wrote about the area he called New England: "Here every man may be a master of his own labor and land in a short time."[1]

Early Settlements

In 1621, King James I granted a large tract between the Merrimack and Piscataqua rivers to Captain John Mason, governor of an area of Canada called Newfoundland. Mason, along with Sir Fernandino Gorges, formed the Laconia Company. It was made up of British merchants who hoped to get rich.

The company supplied settlers with tools, food, and

animals. In 1623, David Thomson, a Scotsman, started a settlement at Pannaway, now the town of Rye. Brothers Edward and Thomas Hilton, fish merchants from London, settled eight miles north at Northam, now called Dover. Both were settled to establish fishing businesses in the New World.

The town of Exeter was settled by the Reverend John Wheelwright and his son. Wheelwright had been banished from Massachusetts Bay Colony because of religious beliefs. He bought land directly from the American Indians.

Use of Timber

Most of New Hampshire was covered with forests, so a timber business began to prosper. Colonists would rather buy timber locally than order it from England.

Much timber was also exported to England. The tall, straight pine trees made ideal masts for the British ships. Eventually, the king had all the best trees marked for his use. Colonists who cut down one of the king's trees paid a heavy fine.

Relations with American Indians

At first, the American Indians taught the Europeans to use plants for medicine, and their trails served as roads. They traded furs for manufactured goods from England. Sometimes, when food was in short supply, the American Indians gave the colonists food.

However, the settlers took advantage of the American Indians, who resented this. Their streams were polluted with sawdust from the colonial mills, and salmon could no longer live there. The English stretched nets across the rivers, keeping the American Indians from fishing there. Lumbering drove the animals that American Indians hunted for food deep into the forests, and the colonists' domestic animals ruined the American Indians' cornfields.

Finally, in 1675, King Philip, son of Massasoit, launched an attack on the Oyster River, where the town of Durham stands today. They burned the houses and killed and captured colonists. This was the beginning of King Philip's War.

After Philip died in 1676, the uprising soon ended. The American Indians signed a treaty with Major Richard Waldron, a militia commander. However, Waldron tricked some of the American Indians into being captured after he had won their confidence. He sold some as slaves, and some died in captivity.

The American Indians retaliated. They killed Waldron and twenty-two other people, and burned their homes to the ground.

New Hampshire Joins Massachusetts Bay

The colony could not agree on a way of government. In 1641, it decided to join the Massachusetts Bay colony for protection. New Hampshire remained a part of that colony for nearly forty years.

In 1679, the king decreed that the settlements in the northeast would become a single province called New England. By then, three thousand people lived in Massachusetts Bay. The people felt that their rights

During colonial times, schoolhouses typically consisted of a single room. There the schoolmaster would educate boys of all ages. Girls were sometimes allowed to attend elementary schools, but only in the summer, or when the boys' classes were not in session.

were being taken away. Reverend Jeremy Belknap wrote: "The press was restrained; liberty of conscience infringed; exorbitant fees and taxes demanded without the voice or consent of the people. . . . Town meetings were prohibited."[2]

In December 1688, King James II fell from power and was forced to flee. New England then went back to being separate colonies. New Hampshire rejoined Massachusetts for a time. In 1690, King Charles II made New Hampshire a separate province.

Further Settlement

In 1717, lieutenant governor John Wentworth encouraged settlement inland. A group of Scottish Presbyterians from Northern Ireland settled in New Hampshire. They brought potatoes and flax seeds to plant, and spinning wheels to spin the flax into linen. Both crops did well. They named their town Londonderry for a town in Ireland.

Benning Wentworth, son of John Wentworth, was named governor in 1741. During his twenty-five year term of office, the colony was beset by trouble with American Indians.

New Hampshire in the French and Indian War

In the early 1750s, there were many attacks against British colonists along the Merrimac and Connecticut rivers. In 1754, a convention of delegates was called. Men from seven colonies planned a defense against the French and American Indians.

Robert Rogers organized a group called Rogers' Rangers. They served as spies and scouts for the British around Lake Champlain. In 1759, they attacked the home base of the St. Francis Indians and destroyed it. Other New Hampshire volunteers captured Crown Point on Lake Champlain.

The Treaty of Paris was finally signed between France and England in 1763. It ended the war and awarded a large amount of land to the British. This included present-day Canada and most of the land east of the Mississippi River in the present-day United States.

Governor Wentworth died in 1766 and was replaced by his nephew, Sir John Wentworth. The new governor was only thirty years old when he took over in 1767, but did a good job of juggling British demands and the colonists' needs. He believed to the end, though, that Britain had the right to rule the colony.

Problems with England

England worried about the growing confidence of the colonies. The mother country started tightening regulations. Colonists were upset by new taxes and the fact that they had no representation. When the Townshend Acts were passed, the dissatisfaction centered in Exeter.

Many of the rich people along the coast were Loyalists (loyal to England), while most farmers in the middle and northern parts of New Hampshire opposed the policies of England. They had little contact with England, and many of them wanted independence.

New Hampshire Colonists Act

When England closed Boston Harbor to punish Massachusetts for the Boston Tea Party, New Hampshire was sympathetic. Its committee of correspondence sent a letter to Boston and donated two hundred British pounds to help the poor.

When the first meeting of the New Hampshire assembly was held, Wentworth tried unsuccessfully to adjourn it. Through a series of meetings of men from all over the colony, a system of government was established. At their first meeting, the colonists elected delegates to the First Continental Congress in Philadelphia.

The Road to Independence

In 1774, three things happened that convinced most New Hampshire citizens that the only choice was independence. First, Governor Wentworth sent carpenters to Boston to work on barracks to house General Gage's troops, without telling them what they would be doing. Next, news came from England that the king would no longer allow the shipment of gunpowder to the colonies.

Finally, Paul Revere rode on December 13 to inform everyone that a British ship was on its way to take over the garrison at Fort William and Mary in Portsmouth. Before the British arrived, four hundred patriots raided the fort and removed one hundred barrels of powder. They also confined the British officer and his men.

On April 19, General Gage tried to take over the provisions and stores in Concord, Massachusetts. Twelve hundred New Hampshire militiamen marched to Boston to help turn back Gage's troops. New Hampshire had entered the Revolutionary War. The colony had come a long way from its early days as a small collection of fishing and timber communities among American Indian villages. Now, the colonists were ready to fight to gain their independence.

NEW YORK

In 1524, Italian explorer Giovanni da Verrazzano, sailing for the French, was first to explore the Hudson River in New York State. He described the land as "a very agreeable situation located within two small prominent hills, in the midst of which flowed to the sea a very big river."[1]

Next to explore the area was Henry Hudson in 1609, and the river bears his name today. An Englishman, Hudson explored for the Dutch. Near present-day Albany, he met some American Indians. According to his English firstmate, Robert Juet, who kept a journal, the American Indians had tobacco, maize, and beaver and otter skins which "wee bought for trifles."[2] He meant that they had traded small trinkets for them. Hudson claimed the land for the Netherlands.

In 1613, the Dutch sent Adriaen Block to explore the area. He built a small fort on Castle Island, near Albany. He called it Nassau. It was flooded out and later replaced by a new fort called Fort Orange.

Permanent Settlements Begin

The Dutch West India Company wanted to establish a fur trade and settle the area. The first colonists settled

American Indians in canoes would greet Henry Hudson's ship the Half Moon *on its way up the Hudson River. The Indians often wanted to trade with the explorers.*

near Fort Orange in 1623. They became friendly with the American Indians and traded with them for furs. Beaver pelts were in great demand, and in the spring, five hundred beaver skins and five hundred otter skins were sent to Holland.

Another group settled on the eastern bank of the Delaware River. They built another fort, and also called it Fort Nassau.

Sources disagree as to whether Manhattan Island was purchased from the American Indians in 1624 by Governor Peter Minuit or by his predecessor, Willem Verhulst. At any rate, the American Indians traded the island to the Dutch for about twenty-four dollars worth of trinkets.

Problems for the Settlers

At first, the settlers lived in trenches dug into the ground with timbers on the sides and roofs made of branches, then covered with turf or bark. In 1625, builders arrived and built better houses. The streets that were laid out then in Fort Amsterdam still exist today.

Soon, trouble broke out with the American Indians at Fort Orange. They had murdered four colonists. Only twenty-five traders remained at Fort Orange, but there were soon two hundred seventy people at Fort Amsterdam.[3]

It was difficult to get people to settle in New Netherland, because life in Holland was quite comfortable. The voyage to the New World was horrible and most people did not want to settle in a faraway land filled with danger.

The Dutch settlers tried unsuccessfully to grow tobacco and to raise silkworms. They finally realized that furs and timbers would bring the most profit.

The Patroon System

The Dutch settlers set up six farms on Manhattan Island to grow food. That helped, but the colony still depended on Holland for some supplies. In 1629, the patroon system was introduced. The West India Company would grant land to any member of the company who paid to send fifty settlers to New Netherland. They had to stay for at least a year. The patroon, or landowner, could choose either sixteen miles along the coast or on one side of a river, or eight miles along both sides of a river.

Five patroonships were created, but only one lasted. Four of the patroons remained in Holland, and it was hard for them to know what was going on.

Problems Between the Dutch and the English

Because of the explorations of John and Sebastian Cabot in 1497, England claimed all of North America. The English were not happy with the colony of New Netherland, which was between their colonies in Virginia and New England.

The Dutch and English had other differences, too. King James I of England proclaimed that no one from any other nation could fish on the coasts and seas of

England. The Dutch had always fished there and made a good profit. They won the conflict because of treaty rights. Then, James decided to make them pay a tax for fishing near England, and they refused. England also told the Dutch to stop whaling near Greenland, which they claimed was English land.

The Dutch did a lot of trading with the Spice Islands, and the English did not like that, either. These islands are located in Indonesia and are now called the Moluccas.

When the Pilgrims lived in Holland, they were close to the Dutch. That relationship did not carry over into the New World, though. The English were afraid that the Dutch would take over most of the fur trade.

Relations Worsen Between the Countries

In 1632, the British seized a Dutch ship that had put into Plymouth Harbor for repairs. When the Dutch demanded its release, they were told that England had claimed all of North America. King Charles told the Dutch in America they might remain as long as they would submit to British government. They refused. Relations between England and Holland became even more strained.

The same year, an entire town on Manhattan was wiped out by American Indians. Rather than taking revenge, Governor Bastiaen Jansz Krol invited the American Indians for talks. His action resulted in a peace treaty.

By 1650, there were about a thousand people in New Amsterdam, and the population doubled in the next ten years.

Only two-thirds of the colonists in New Netherland were Dutch. There were British from Connecticut, Germans, French, Finns, and Jews. Swedes lived along the Delaware River, and there were a number of slaves in the colony, as well.

Settlers Unhappy

The settlers were unhappy under the rule of the Dutch. They were not allowed any say in their government. Holland was more concerned with making money from the fur trade than with the happiness of the settlers.

Peter Stuyvesant was governor from 1647 to 1664. He was unpopular with colonists.

England Takes Over New Netherland

Charles II was now King of England. He decided to take over the colony. He awarded "all the land from the west side of the Connectecutte River to the East side of De la Ware Bay" to his brother, James, the Duke of York.[4] He gave James the authority to govern the inhabitants.

Charles sent four warships to seize New Netherland. Stuyvesant heard that they were coming, and tore up the letters asking him to surrender. The colonists refused to fight the English, so he was forced to give up. The Dutch were granted religious freedom and full property and inheritance rights.

New Netherland Becomes New York

The duke renamed the city New York. He appointed officials, controlled trade, granted land, and directed defense. He told his governors to treat the people well. He

On September 8, 1664, the English officially took over New Amsterdam from the Dutch. Here, Peter Stuyvesant (standing, with wooden leg), surrenders the colony.

appointed local citizens to the governor's council in order to learn local opinions.

The Duke of York ruled the colony for twenty-one years before he became King James II. He then ruled for another three years as king. In 1686, he created the Dominion of New England, which was governed by Edmund Andros.

Changes in British Rule

When Parliament offered the throne to his Protestant daughter, Mary, and her husband, William III, James was forced to flee.

A group of merchants under Jacob Leisler ruled the colony of New York for a short time until William and Mary abandoned plans for the Dominion of New England in 1688. They made New York a royal colony again.

The people were allowed to take part in their government. The assembly steadily gained power throughout the 1700s, and the governors became less powerful. The colonists wanted more self-government, and resented rule by England.

The French and Indian War

New York was very involved in the French and Indian War. The colony was open to attack because it was so close to Canada. The French had built forts on Lakes Champlain, Ontario, and Erie.

In July 1758, the British attacked the French at Fort Ticonderoga. Although the British troops outnumbered the French fifteen thousand to three thousand, they lost the battle. The French mowed down the redcoats as they marched toward the fort. The British lost 1,600 men and the British colonists 334.

Seven weeks later, the British captured Fort Frontenac, on the northeastern corner of Lake Ontario. On July 25, 1759, the British attacked and occupied Fort Niagara. That broke France's link between Lake Ontario and Lake Erie. On October 12, the British defeated the French fleet on Lake Champlain. Now the British controlled the waters between Canada and New York.

The British took Montreal on September 8, and the French gave up. The French and Indian War was over.

Resentment Develops Against the British Government

Most New York colonists resented providing quarters for British soldiers during the war. They were still clamoring for self-government. They resented the Stamp Act, the Townshend Acts, the tax on tea, and other taxes.

When the British closed Boston Harbor and Massachusetts colonists lost any say in their government, the New Yorkers thought that they could be next. The assembly had appointed a committee of correspondence in 1755 to communicate with other colonies. In January 1774, a new committee was established.

Paving the Way for Independence

In September 1774, the colonists sent delegates to a meeting of all the colonies in Philadelphia. This First

SOURCE DOCUMENT

... FROM AND AFTER THE FIRST DAY OF DECEMBER NEXT, WE WILL NOT IMPORT, INTO BRITISH AMERICA, FROM GREAT-BRITAIN OR IRELAND, ANY GOODS, WARES, OR MERCHANDISE WHATSOEVER, OR FROM ANY OTHER PLACE, ANY SUCH GOODS, WARES, OR MERCHANDISE, AS SHALL HAVE BEEN EXPORTED FROM GREAT-BRITAIN OR IRELAND; NOR WILL WE, AFTER THAT DAY, IMPORT ANY EAST-INDIA TEA FROM ANY PART OF THE WORLD; NOR ANY MOLASSES, SYRUPS, PANELES, COFFEE, OR PIMENTO, FROM THE BRITISH PLANTATIONS OR FROM DOMINICA; NOR WINES FROM MADEIRA, OR THE WESTERN ISLANDS; NOR FOREIGN INDIGO.[5]

The Continental Association brought New York and the other colonies one step closer to revolution.

Continental Congress adopted the "Continental Association," an agreement not to trade with Britain until American rights were restored.

When New York heard of the Battles of Lexington and Concord, the leaders were ready for action. A voluntary force was raised and armed with six hundred muskets they had seized from a British government arsenal.

Less than a month after Lexington and Concord, Fort Ticonderoga fell to the colonials. Ethan Allen led the group, called the Green Mountain Boys, on the surprise attack. A band of New Englanders took Crown Point two days later. The New Yorkers were in the thick of the Revolution.

NEW JERSEY

New Jersey was settled by small numbers of people from many countries, and the growth of the colony was very slow.

The Lenni Lenape Indians were in the New Jersey area long before Giovanni de Verrazzano, an Italian exploring for France, became the first European to explore the area in 1524. In 1609, Henry Hudson claimed all the land in the area for the Dutch. He was probably the first white man to set foot on the Jersey shore when he anchored in Sandy Hook Bay. The first mate, Robert Juet, wrote "This day the people of the country came aboard of us, seemingly very glad of our coming."[1]

Early Settlement in New Jersey

Michael Pauw was granted a large area of land across from Manhattan Island in 1630. He was to bring in new settlers, but made little effort. He named the settlement Pavonia. Only two houses were built. A few settlers moved onto scattered homesteads in the next few years. Pauw lost interest and gave up his claim.

In 1638, a Swedish expedition under Peter Minuit arrived to start a colony on the Delaware River. That year, he built Fort Christina, which was named after the young Swedish queen. In 1643, Fort Nya Elfsborg was built on the Jersey shore of the river. It was soon abandoned, however, due to swarms of mosquitoes.

The Swedes built the first log cabins in North America along the Delaware River. Swedish settlers got little backing from their government, and most Swedes were not interested in colonizing a wilderness so far from home. New Sweden never had more than four hundred settlers.

The First American Indian Attacks

In 1641, the Mahican Indians from the north attacked the tribes around Pavonia. They killed seventeen settlers and seized some of the women and children. Most of the remaining colonists fled to Manhattan. By February 1643, only ten settlers remained in Pavonia.

William Kieft, director general of New Netherland, sent a force to attack the Mahicans and killed eighty of them near Pavonia. The American Indians retaliated by destroying all the farms from Pavonia to the Connecticut Valley.

The Dutch Take Over

Peter Stuyvesant took over as director-general in New Netherland in 1647. For the next few years, many Dutch settlers migrated to the Pavonia area and started new settlements.

The Dutch believed they owned the area around the Delaware River. By 1655, Stuyvesant forced the Swedish to surrender the land. The New Jersey area became part

The early settlers of New Jersey frequently had to deal with American Indian attacks. The Indians did not like the fact that their land was being taken away from them.

of New Netherland. The Swedes were allowed to either remain or return to Sweden.

In March 1660, the Dutch settled Bergen, the first permanent town in New Jersey. It was surrounded by palisades (fences made of large pointed sticks) to protect the residents from American Indian attack. The next year, the town was allowed to govern itself and was given its own court.

The English Takeover

The 1660s were hard years for the Dutch in all New Netherland. They were constantly pressured by the English in New England, who did not recognize their claim to the land. Money was scarce and the people were unhappy. As a result, the English took over without opposition in 1664.

After the takeover, many Dutch moved from New York into New Jersey. Meanwhile, the Duke of York had given New Jersey to two friends, Sir George Carteret and John, Lord Berkeley. They owned the land and assumed they could govern it as they saw fit. They hoped to get a good income from the property.

Governing the Colony

The duke had already sent Colonel Richard Nicholls to govern the colony. Because Nicholls did not know that the duke had given land to his friends, he granted some of the same land to settlers. Many were Baptists from Rhode Island and Quakers from Long Island.

Berkeley and Carteret sent Carteret's cousin, Captain Philip Carteret, to serve as governor in the area. He arrived in 1665 and chose Elizabethtown as the capital.

Lord Berkeley and George Carteret, drew up a constitution called the Concessions and Agreements for New Jersey in 1665. This was the beginning of self-government in the colony. The freeholders in each town met on January 1 to elect two delegates to an assembly.

These delegates, along with the governor and his appointed council, made the laws. The council had the power to set up courts, provide for defense, and enact a criminal code. No taxes could be levied except by the general assembly. Laws needed to be consistent with those of England and approved by the proprietors.

SOURCE DOCUMENT

III. ITEM. TO EVERY FFREEMAN [SIC] AND FFREEWOMAN [SIC] [WHO] SHALL ARRIVE IN THE SAID PROVINCE, ARMED AND PROVIDED AS AFORESAID WITHIN THE SECOND YEAR FROM THE FIRST DAY OF JANUARY 1665 TO THE FIRST OF JAN'Y [SIC] 1966 WITH AN INTENC'ON [SIC] TO PLANT 90 ACRES OF LAND ENGLISH MEASURE, AND FOR EVERY ABLE MAN SERVANT THAT HEE [SIC] OR SHE SHALL CARRY OR SEND ARMED AND PROVIDED AS AFORESAID 90 ACRES OF LAND LIKE MEASURE.[2]

Under the Concessions and Agreements for New Jersey, each colonist received ninety acres of land to farm.

Quitrents and New Settlement

When settlers received a grant for land, they did not own it outright. They were to pay what was known as a quitrent. Each year, they paid a halfpenny or a penny an acre for it. This caused discontent among the colonists. Those who had earlier purchased land from the American Indians thought it should not apply to them. The first payments of quitrents were not due until 1670.

Puritans settled along the Passaic River. They called their settlement New Ark, later to become Newark.

In 1670 when the first quitrents came due, most settlers refused to pay them. In May 1672, an illegal assembly met at Elizabethtown. They removed Philip Carteret from his job as governor and elected the son of the proprietor, James Carteret, as "President of the Country." Philip Carteret returned to England to find out what to do. In New Jersey history, this has been called the "Revolution of 1672."

Dutch Rule Again Briefly

In 1673, during a war between England and Holland, a Dutch ship sailed into New York Harbor and took control there. For almost a year, the Dutch ruled again, until the English won the war. Dutch rule had little effect on the colonists. After the war, the proprietors went back to running New Jersey, and Philip Carteret was restored to his position as governor.

Ownership Changes

Lord Berkeley sold his interest in New Jersey to a group of Quakers, members of the Society of Friends, a peace-loving religion. The Quinipartite Deed in July 1676 divided the colony into East Jersey and West Jersey. East Jersey still belonged to Sir George Carteret, and West Jersey became the property of the Quaker group.

In 1680, Sir Edmund Andros, governor of New York, took over the government of New Jersey. Soldiers seized Philip Carteret and took him to New York, where he was put on trial for wrongfully ruling over New Jersey. A jury found him not guilty.

In March, word came from England that the duke disagreed with Andros's actions and Carteret was again back in power. Sir George Carteret had amended the constitution, and the representatives said he had no right to do that. Finally, he dissolved the assembly in East Jersey.

The next year, Sir George Carteret died and East Jersey was put up for public auction. A group of twelve men, including William Penn of the colony of Pennsylvania, bought it. Twelve more joined them, and they became known as the "Twenty-Four Proprietors."

Barclay Becomes Governor

The new governor was Robert Barclay, a Scottish Quaker. He encouraged Scots to settle in East Jersey, but only about five hundred came. East Jersey now had about five thousand people. Two-thirds lived in the seven towns, and the others lived on farms. There was little trade and no industry. Agriculture was the only business. The colonists grew wheat, corn, oats, flax, barley, and vegetables.

New Jersey Becomes a Royal Colony

In 1702, New Jersey became a royal colony and East and West Jersey were reunited. New Jersey shared a governor with New York, but kept its own assembly. In 1738, New Jerseyites were finally given their own governor, making New Jersey an independent colony.

Dissatisfaction with the British Government

As in the other colonies, there was unrest in New Jersey through the late 1760s and 1770s. Benjamin Franklin's son, William, was governor. Although he had solved several difficult problems and most people respected him, hostility mounted toward William Franklin.

The colonists resented the Quartering Act, which instructed colonial assemblies to furnish supplies to British troops in the area. The assembly voted in 1771 to cut off funds for the barracks. Governor Franklin did not know what to do, so he ended the session of the assembly.

When they learned that the royal troops in New Jersey had been moved to East Florida, the assembly members were finally convinced to vote to pay back the British commander the personal money he had spent on supplies.

New Jersey was one of the smaller colonies. It did not have the same degree of discontent with England that was seen in Virginia and Massachusetts. Many New Jerseyans were finally driven to protest when the Coercive Acts (also called the Intolerable Acts) were passed in 1774. In June, New Jersey formed local committees of correspondence to demand that the Boston Port Act be repealed and call for a continental congress. They also sent delegates to the congress.

The New Jersey assembly met in January 1775. Franklin advised them to draw up a list of grievances, which he would personally present to the king. The assembly appointed the same delegates to attend the Second Continental Congress, which would meet in May.

Getting Ready for War

When news came in April of the Battles of Lexington and Concord, the New Jersey men began drilling. It was rumored that British ships off Sandy Hook were preparing to raid New Jersey.

New Jersey's first provincial congress met on May 23, 1775, in Trenton. The congress pledged allegiance to the king, but resolved to keep up correspondence with the other colonies. It decided that every township should raise a company of volunteers, and a tax was levied to pay for them.

The Second Continental Congress was meeting at the time. New Jersey's second provincial congress met on January 31, 1776. A majority of the delegates were now in favor of independence. On July 2, New Jersey adopted its state constitution.

MARYLAND

Chesapeake Bay was first explored by Captain John Smith in 1608, but the colony of Maryland was not officially started until 1634. In 1628, William Claiborne discovered and explored Palmer's Island and Kent Island, just off the coast of present-day Annapolis. Claiborne, secretary of the Virginia colony, started a trading post on Kent Island.

In 1632, King Charles granted a large tract of land north of the Potomac River to George Calvert, former British secretary of state, who was the first Lord Baltimore. George Calvert had visited Virginia and wanted to start a new colony. Calvert died before he could settle the land, but his son, Cecilius, the second Lord Baltimore, carried out his wishes.

Maryland Is Settled

Lord Baltimore, Cecilius Calvert, was not interested in establishing a Roman Catholic colony, even though he was Catholic. He saw Maryland as a settlement open to people of all religious faiths on equal terms.[1]

The charter the king granted Calvert was very liberal. The people would enjoy "all the privileges, franchises, and liberties" of English subjects, the crown would levy no taxes on persons or goods in the colony, and laws would be made "by the proprietor, with the advice . . . of the freemen of the colony."[2] The laws were to be "consonant to reason, and . . . agreeeable [sic] to the laws of England."[3]

In return, Lord Baltimore would pay a fifth of any precious metals mined to the crown, as well as sending two arrowheads each year to the King as a token of loyalty. Maryland was the first colony run by a proprietor.

Lord Baltimore named his brother, Leonard Calvert, governor of the new colony. Governor Calvert and about three hundred settlers reached Maryland in March 1634. They built a town called St. Mary's on a small island at the mouth of the Potomac River. They paid the American Indians for the land with hoes, axes, and cloth. Most of the settlers farmed, and tobacco soon became the biggest cash crop.

Confrontation with Claiborne

William Claiborne was not pleased when he learned Kent Island would be under the government of Maryland. In 1635, a battle occurred in which several men were killed. Two years later, Claiborne went back to England to unsuccessfully plead his case with the king. When he returned, he found that the Maryland settlers had taken over Kent Island. He went to Virginia, but continued to cause problems for Governor Calvert over the next twenty years.

Problems in England

In England, there was a struggle between Parliament and the king. In 1645, Richard Ingle, a Parliament sympathizer, seized control of Maryland. This is known as Ingle's Rebellion. By the next year, Calvert had regained control.

On April 21, 1649, the Maryland assembly passed an Act Concerning Religion, also known as the Religious Toleration Act. It guaranteed freedom of religion for all Christian denominations, but did not tolerate those who were not Christians. Anyone who did not believe in the Trinity (God the father, Jesus the son, and the Holy Spirit) could be put to death. So, while liberal by seventeenth century standards, the Religious Toleration Act would not be considered liberal today.

That year, Charles I was beheaded by Parliament forces, and they took over the government of England. England was ruled for the next nine years by Oliver Cromwell, leader of the rebellion.

Changes in Government of Maryland

William Stone became governor in 1649. However, Parliament took over Maryland, throwing Governor Stone out of office in 1652. He raised a small army and, in 1655, met the Puritans in battle at Providence, where Annapolis is now located.

Stone was defeated in what became known as the Battle of Severn, and the Puritans retained control. They suspended the Toleration Act and denied religious freedom to Baptists, Quakers, Catholics, and Episcopalians.

Cromwell thought that the Puritans went too far, and he restored the Toleration Act. He also made Lord Baltimore proprietor again. In 1661, Lord Baltimore sent his son, Charles Calvert, to be governor. He had served fourteen years when his father died, making him Lord Baltimore and proprietor of the colony. This was the first time the proprietor had lived in the colony.

The time from 1661 to 1688 was unusually peaceful and quiet. Most settlers were happy and the population was growing. Quakers, Dutch, Germans, and Huguenots came to Maryland.

In 1688, William of Orange, a Protestant, became King of England. At that time, the Protestant majority in Maryland took over the colony. William appointed a governor in 1691, and Maryland remained a royal colony until 1715. The Church of England was the official religion, but other religions were tolerated.

The capital of Maryland was moved from the Catholic St. Mary's City to the Protestant town of Annapolis in 1694.

Charles Calvert was serving as governor of Maryland when he also became the new Lord Baltimore and proprietor of the colony.

The Calverts in Control Again

In 1715, the fourth Lord Baltimore, Benedict Calvert, converted from Catholicism to the Church of England. He was given control over Maryland. The Calverts remained in control until the American Revolution.

Disagreements over the boundary between Maryland and Pennsylvania were not finally settled until the Mason-Dixon Line was established in 1767. Some of the land Lord Baltimore had given to others was later granted to William Penn as part of his territory, causing the dispute.

Discontent With British Rule

Throughout the 1760s, there was discontent between the proprietors and the colonists. The people wanted more power, and their assembly gained power as time went by. During the French and Indian War, the government of Maryland had refused to help the British government. They resented it when Parliament then taxed them to help pay the cost of the war.

Maryland was one of the first colonies to lend its support for independence. The people of Frederick County protested the Stamp Act in 1765. In 1774, Maryland had its own tea party, when colonists burned a tea ship, the *Peggy Stewart*, in Annapolis. Maryland was ready for independence when the Declaration of Independence was approved.

8

CONNECTICUT

The name Connecticut comes from an American Indian word, *Quinatuc-quet*, meaning "beside the long tidal river."[1]

Adriaen Block was first to explore the Connecticut River when he discovered it in 1614. Dutch traders founded trading posts near present-day Hartford that same year, but did not make any permanent settlements.

First Permanent Settlement

Puritans in England were persecuted because of their attempts to purify the Church of England. They wanted the church to consist of simple services, Bible study, and sermons on moral duty.

In 1636, Thomas Hooker, a Puritan minister, brought a group of colonists from Massachusetts. They founded the town of Hartford.

Hooker's group bought land from the American Indians, who taught them farming, hunting, and fishing techniques. That same year, the Pequot attacked an English fort at Saybrook.

In 1637, a group of ninety settlers under Captain John Mason wiped out the Pequot fort at Mystic, killing over six hundred Pequot and capturing others. The captives were given to friendly tribes to serve as slaves.

More Settlers Arrive

That same year, Reverend John Davenport and Theophilus Eaton brought two boatloads of Puritans from England to Boston. The settlers did not like it there, so in April 1638, they relocated to Connecticut. They then formed the New Haven Colony.

African Americans in Connecticut

Slavery began early in Connecticut. Many of the prominent early settlers, such as Davenport and Eaton, owned slaves. Ships brought the Africans into Connecticut ports. Some were bought, and others were sent to southern plantations. The average slaveholder in Connecticut only owned one to three slaves. There was not as great a need for their labor as there was in the South, because there were no big plantations in the northern colonies.

Slaves had few rights, and even free blacks were not treated as equals. They had to carry passes when they left their towns. They could not serve on juries, vote, or hold office, but free blacks had to pay taxes.

Connecticut Receives Royal Charter

In 1662, Hartford and New Haven were combined under a royal charter to make Connecticut. However, in 1687, the English governor, Sir Edmund Andros, was told by King James II to take the charter.

An assembly was called to discuss the matter. But during the talks, all the candles were suddenly blown out. When they were relighted, the charter was gone. According to legend, Captain Wadsworth of Hartford

The Charter Oak (left) became an important symbol in Connecticut history.

took the charter and placed it in a large hollow oak tree so Andros could not get it. This tree has been known as the Charter Oak ever since.

Puritans Intolerant of Other Religions

The Puritans had left England because they wanted religious freedom, but they were not willing to grant the same freedom to others. They expected everyone to join the Congregational Church.

Quakers settled in Connecticut in the seventeenth century. They disagreed with the Puritan religion and refused to pay titles, take oaths, or fight. They were often punished with heavy fines or whippings. Some were cast out to Rhode Island, where their beliefs were accepted.

A Baptist Church was started in Groton in 1705. The Baptists were also harassed by Puritan authorities. They remained quiet and their numbers began to grow. Baptist churches started in other towns.

Laws and Education

Connecticut had harsh laws, including the death penalty for many offenses. People thought to be witches were prosecuted in Connecticut. Alice Young of Windsor was the first to be executed for witchcraft in 1647. Ten more people were executed during 1662 and 1663.

Education started early in Connecticut so children would be able to read the Bible. The Code of 1650 required towns of at least fifty families to hire a teacher to teach reading and writing. Larger towns had to have schools that would prepare students for college.

Connecticut was made up of isolated rural communities. The Puritan clergy ruled. This was the only colony that did not follow English practices in legislature, or base its legal code on English law. Therefore, Connecticut settlers did not like the British making laws for them.

Connecticut was in poor economic shape in 1764. The colony had spent 260,000 pounds during the French and Indian War. It had also sent five thousand men into battle.

Dissatisfaction with the British

When the Sugar Act was passed in 1764, the colonists were upset that it would cut off the major source of trade with the West Indies. Colonial Governor Thomas Fitch sent an official protest to London. The British ignored the protest and passed the Stamp Act in 1765. Western settlers figured they could do nothing but accept them. Eastern settlers were outraged and vowed to take action.

Colonists Make Their Feelings Known

The colonists staged a fiery demonstration on August 22, 1765, in New London. In a speech, Dr. Benjamin Church condemned Jared Ingersoll. Ingersoll was a stampmaster, enforcing the Stamp Act. He was hung in effigy (a dummy representing him was hung) by the crowd. Protest meetings followed.

That summer, some of eastern Connecticut's most distinguished leaders started the Sons of Liberty. They wanted to try to convince Connecticut residents that they could only be free if they got rid of the Tory leaders, who were loyal to England. They also organized the colony to elect patriotic leaders.

A group of one thousand colonists, armed with clubs, stopped Ingersoll and got him to resign. In the next election those who wanted independence won. Many Connecticut colonists supported the Boston Tea Party in 1773. Connecticut promised aid for Boston and established a committee of correspondence to keep in touch with patriots in other colonies, as the Revolutionary War approached.

RHODE ISLAND

The first confirmed visit to Rhode Island was in 1524 by Giovanni da Verrazzano. He first found Block Island, off the Rhode Island Coast.

Verrazzano described Narragansett Harbor near Rhode Island as "a very large bay twenty leagues (about sixty miles) in circumference, in which are five small islands of great fertility and beauty, covered with large and tall trees. . . . South toward the harbour entrance on both sides are very pleasant hills and many clear streams flowing down to the sea."[1]

The area was inhabited by Wampanoag Indians, members of the Algonquin tribe. Pequot Indians lived further north. They grew crops, fished, hunted, and gathered nuts and berries. They made tools and weapons from stone, and wove baskets and nets from reeds.

Adriaen Block visited Rhode Island next. He was sent in 1614 by the Amsterdam Company to explore the area. The Block Island Indians welcomed him.

William Blackstone, a minister who disagreed with the church in Massachusetts, was the first permanent settler in Rhode Island. He arrived in 1635 and built a house.

Williams Considered the Founder

Roger Williams, who arrived in 1636, is credited with founding Rhode Island. A nonconformist who disagreed with the Puritans, as well as the Church of England, he and his wife, Mary, had come to Massachusetts in 1631. He served as an assistant pastor in Boston. Williams showed a great interest in the American Indians, learning their customs and language and trying to convert them to Christianity.

Williams's Problems with the Puritans

The Puritans were rigid and intolerant, and Williams was not popular among them. He was open in his criticism of England and the Massachusetts Bay colony. He said the colony's land belonged to the American Indians, and the king had no right to claim it. Williams believed in religious freedom. In 1635, he was found guilty of spreading dangerous ideas and banished from the colony.

The Puritans planned to send Williams back to England, so he fled into the wilderness in a near-blizzard. He fought his way across a swamp, through the snow and thick trees, and crossed icy streams. He wrote, "I was sorely tossed for . . . fourteen weeks in bitter winter season, not knowing what bread or bed did mean."[2] Williams finally found shelter with the American Indians at the headquarters of Chief Massasoit.

Rhode Island Under Williams

Williams bought land from the American Indians and started Providence. Other settlers came from Salem and Boston. They signed a "town fellowship" agreement, which guaranteed religious freedom for all.

Life was hard. Land had to be cleared and planted. The Rhode Islanders lived in hillside dugouts until they could build houses.

The surrounding land provided a variety of food for the colonists. They depended on venison (deer meat) and wild fowl for meat. Because of the nearby ocean, fish and shellfish were plentiful. Nuts and berries were gathered in the inland woods. However, food was still scarce the first winter.

The American Indians were friendly, often visiting and bringing food. The crops did well. The temperature in Rhode Island was milder than in other parts of New England.

SOURCE DOCUMENT

WE WHOSE NAMES ARE HEREUNDER, DESIROUS TO INHABIT IN THE TOWN OF PROVIDENCE, DO PROMISE TO SUBJECT OURSELVES IN ACTIVE AND PASSIVE OBEDIENCE TO ALL SUCH ORDERS OR AGREEMENTS AS SHALL BE MADE FOR THE PUBLIC GOOD OF THE BODY IN AN ORDERLY WAY, BY THE MAJOR CONSENT OF PRESENT INHABITANTS, MASTERS OF FAMILIES, INCORPORATED TOGETHER IN A TOWNE FELLOWSHIP, AND OTHERS WHOM THEY SHALL ADMIT UNTO THEM ONLY IN CIVIL THINGS.[3]

Signed on August 20, 1637, the Providence Agreement ensured that only laws that a majority of the people favored could me passed in the town. The agreement also was the first colonial attempt at separation of church (religion) and state (the government).

Williams Keeps the American Indians Happy

There was an American Indian war in 1637, but Providence was not targeted. Williams learned that representatives of the Pequot Indian tribe were trying to convince the Narragansett to join them in fighting the settlers. Williams paddled across the bay and joined the meeting. He listened carefully, then addressed them in their own language. The Narragansett decided to remain neutral.

Williams tried to avoid war by talking to the Massachusetts colonial leaders. They promised to spare the women and children when they raided the Pequot camp. Instead, they burned the village with everyone in it and killed those who ran out.

Williams was upset that they had broken their promise. Massachusetts had problems with many American Indian uprisings over the years, but Rhode Island lived in relative peace.

Anne Hutchinson Settles Portsmouth

In 1638, Portsmouth was settled. Anne Hutchinson settled there with her husband, William, and their sixteen children. She had been tried in Boston for heresy (speaking against the Church's beliefs) and banished from Massachusetts. She did not believe in the rituals of the Puritan church. She said the church had no right to force people to go to church or to oversee their morals.

The same year, Reverend John Clarke and William Coddington, who had supported Anne Hutchinson, were forced to leave Boston. They bought land from the

American Indians and started a new settlement on Aquidneck Island.

The town of Warwick was founded in 1643. Three years later, Roger Williams moved his family there and started a trading post.

Rhode Island Receives Royal Patent

The people of Rhode Island worried that Massachusetts might try to take over their land. Williams went to London where he received a royal patent for Rhode Island in March 1644. The patent read, in part, "The Providence Plantations in the Narragansett Bay" were to "govern and rule themselves by such form of civil government by voluntary consent of all, or the greater part of them."[4] This made Rhode Island an independent colony, and gave it more freedom than most of the colonies enjoyed.

A code of laws drawn up in 1647 was very modern for the times. The towns of Providence, Portsmouth, Newport, and Warwick each sent six representatives to a general court.

The first African slaves arrived in Rhode Island in 1652. Also in 1652, Williams and Clarke sailed to London to obtain an order reaffirming the 1644 patent. Williams became president of the colony in 1654 and served three terms.

Religious Tolerance in Rhode Island

Rhode Island was becoming a refuge for people of many different religions. In 1657, the first Quakers came to

Rhode Island. Williams did not agree with their beliefs, but welcomed them anyway. They were given complete freedom to practice their religion. So were Jewish colonists, who arrived the next year from Holland. Baptists who were persecuted in Massachusetts also found a welcome there.

When King Charles II was restored to the throne, the people of Rhode Island feared for their colony. Clarke had stayed in London to obtain a new charter on July 8, 1663. The charter called for a democratic government and complete religious freedom. However, it did not allow Jews and Catholics to vote.

Both Massachusetts and Plymouth claimed the eastern part of Rhode Island, including Aquidneck Island. In 1665, a royal commission fixed the boundary.

King Philip's War in Rhode Island

During King Philip's War, Williams tried to convince the chief of the Narragansett, Canonchet, to remain neutral. Canonchet assured Williams that they would not harm one hair of his head.[5] But the chief could not be talked out of attacking Providence, where many of the homes were burned. Canonchet was finally captured in Connecticut and executed. His head was sent to Hartford, where it was mounted on a post.

Events of the Late 1600s

In 1685, when King James II revoked the charters of the northern colonies, Rhode Island refused to turn in its charter. In 1689, James II was overthrown. When

William of Orange took his place, the individual colonies went back to their original governments and Governor Andros was jailed in Boston.

In 1696, the first full shipload of African slaves arrived in Newport. Slave trade became the most profitable trade for the colonies. Americans shipped rum from Rhode Island to Africa to buy slaves, they sold the Africans to the West Indies, and with the profit, bought sugar and molasses to make more rum. This was called the Triangular Trade.

Some slaves were used by the large plantations in the western part of Rhode Island. They raised mainly sheep and cattle, and produced butter and cheese. Newport was the busiest port in the Americas. Shipbuilding was an important industry there, too.

Resentment Toward England

The colonists were used to governing themselves, so when England began imposing taxes in the 1760s, they resented it. They felt that because Rhode Islanders did not have representation in Parliament, England had no right to tax them.

England restricted the colonies from manufacturing woolen goods, hats, and iron. The colonies often ignored the order, but they still could not export the products they made.

As the Sugar Act, the Stamp Act, and the Townshend Acts were passed, many Rhode Islanders began to boycott British goods.

The Gaspee *Incident was a product of the Rhode Islanders'
anger toward Britain.*

Steps to Revolution

In 1772, a British ship, the *Gaspee*, ran aground near
Warwick. A group of colonists got the people off the
ship, then set it afire.

Rhode Island reacted quickly to the news of
Lexington and Concord. On May 4, 1776, Rhode Island
declared its independence from England. Militia had
been training on the Commons, and two regiments
marched north to join the new army in Boston. For
Rhode Island, the Revolutionary War had begun.

In 1609, Henry Hudson claimed the area that became Delaware for Holland. The next year, Sir Samuel Argall, a British captain, sailed into Delaware Bay. He named Cape La Warre after the governor of Virginia, Baron De la Warr. The

DELAWARE

Delaware River and colony of Delaware eventually took their names from him as well.

Conflicting Claims

The Dutch and the English both claimed the area. The first attempt at settlement was in 1631, when a group of Dutchmen settled on Lewes Creek. Their town, called Zwaanendael, was located where the town of Lewes is now.

A Colony Wiped Out

The Lenni Lenape Indians had lived peacefully for many years in Delaware. About thirty colonists settled in Zwaanendael. A misunderstanding about a coat of arms posted by the Dutch led to a bloody end to the colony at the hands of the American Indians. Captain David Pietersen de Vries returned the next year to find the bones and skulls of the settlers scattered over the ground.

Hudson learned from some of the American Indians

that a chief had taken the coat of arms, wanting to use the metal to make pipes. The Dutch were very upset. No one is sure what happened next. One story says that other American Indians killed the chief so as not to offend the Dutch. Others say Giles Hossett, the leader of the colony, killed the chief. Whatever happened, the American Indians wiped out the settlement in a bloody massacre.[1]

Swedes Settle in Delaware

No more attempts were made at settling the area until 1638, when a group of Swedes settled where Wilmington now stands. The year before, an expedition headed by Peter Minuit had explored the area for Sweden. Their settlement was called Fort Christina. The first families arrived in 1640 and called the area New Sweden. Many of the colonists in the next few years were not Swedes at all, but were Finns from the neighboring country of Finland.

New Life for the Colony

Colonel Johan Printz arrived in New Sweden in 1643 with food supplies, clothing, guns, livestock, and more colonists and soldiers. This breathed new life into the struggling colony. He served as governor for ten years.

Many settlers died during the early years, often from lack of food. Therefore, Printz made farming a priority. The tobacco plantation he established was a disaster, so the next year they went back to growing corn. The biggest problem was lack of labor. By 1647, there were only 183 settlers in New Sweden.

The Dutch Intrude

The Dutch built Fort Beversreede on the east side of the Schuylkill River in 1648, then abandoned it three years later when they built Fort Casimir where New Castle now stands. Peter Stuyvesant, governor of New Netherland, moved Dutch cannons and ammunition to Fort Casimir.

Printz and the Swedish were outraged, but the Dutch were stronger at the time than the Swedish. People were tired of Printz's strict rule, and in 1653, twenty-two men filed a petition against him. Printz called it a mutiny, and returned to Sweden.

Under Dutch Rule

The population of New Sweden had dropped to seventy. Stuyvesant arrived in 1655 with 317 soldiers and seven armed ships. The Swedes had no choice but to surrender, and New Sweden fell under Dutch rule. A few Swedes went back to Sweden, but most stayed.

A town developed near Fort Casimir. Named New Amstel, it became the capital. The Swedes and Finns actually did well under Dutch rule. It was now easier to secure supplies. In the spring of 1656, a ship brought one hundred more Swedes and Finns. The first schoolmaster arrived in 1658 and set up a school for twenty-five students in New Amstel.

Problems in Delaware

However, there were still problems in the colony. Heavy rain ruined the crops and there was little food. An epidemic of fever killed several people. A ship from Holland brought new settlers, but no food. The colony was nearing starvation. Governor Jacob Alrichs wrote to Stuyvesant that they could only be kept from starvation by food from New Amsterdam.

Meanwhile, agents from Lord Baltimore came into the colony from Maryland and threatened the settlers that the English were about to take over. Many colonists fled to Virginia or Maryland.

The Delaware area never had a strong governor under either the Swedish or the Dutch. Therefore, the colonists there were more independent than in many of the other colonies.

The English thought that the Dutch were intruding in their territory. King Charles II wanted the east coast of America to be under English control. He granted the land in Delaware, New York, and New Jersey to his brother James, the Duke of York.

The English Take Over

The duke sent Richard Nicolls and two warships to take over New Netherland. He told Stuyvesant that the Dutch were trespassing on English territory. He asked them to surrender in the name of Charles II, King of England. Stuyvesant surrendered when his people refused to resist the English takeover.

In Delaware, they did not give up so easily. The English demanded that New Amstel surrender to them. They resisted, and the English fired, killing three of the twenty soldiers who resisted and injuring many more.

The rest of the soldiers and many of the citizens of New Amstel were sold in Virginia as slaves.

In 1671, the first English census of Delaware showed 165 households.

Delaware Under English Rule

The duke ruled the territory from New York City to Delaware. He set up courts and allowed trial by jury. He also allowed complete religious freedom. However, his main purpose was to make money, and he taxed imports and exports. Now that Delaware was under English rule, more people from the other English colonies settled there.

England and Holland were again at war in the 1670s. In August 1673, Dutch ships sailed into New York Harbor and took over the city. For about a year, the Dutch again ruled the area. The Treaty of Westminster, in 1674, restored New Netherland to the English and Major Edmund Andros became governor.

Things were calm for the next six years, and the settlers along the Delaware were comfortable. Their farms were successful and hunting and fishing were good.

Quakers Come to Delaware

About this time in England, the Society of Friends, its followers known as Quakers, was growing. Quakers, like many dissenters, defied the Church of England and met anyway. They refused to pay tithes (money to the church), take oaths, or obey laws they believed were wrong.

William Penn was a Quaker whose father had lent a large sum of money to King Charles. When his father died, Penn asked the king to grant him land in America instead of repaying the money. In 1681, the King gave him land north of Maryland and west of the Delaware River. This was the largest land grant to an individual—larger than the whole country of Ireland. Penn had absolute power to govern the area as he liked, as long as he followed English laws.

William Penn's Holy Experiment

Penn called his colony a "Holy Experiment." He wanted it to be a refuge for Quakers and other people persecuted for religious beliefs.

Penn wrote a constitution allowing freedom of worship and speech and trial by jury. It was the most liberal charter of any of the colonies.

In 1681, Delaware was still part of New York, although it was separated from the rest of the colony by New Jersey. Penn asked the Duke of York to give up claim to Delaware. In 1682, the duke sold Penn the area of Delaware.

Penn said the residents of the three Delaware counties would enjoy all

Delaware became William Penn's "Holy Experiment."

the same privileges as the people of Pennsylvania. He was not as strict as most royal governors. However, the people in the Three Lower Counties of Delaware wanted to continue managing their affairs as they had done for years. In April 1704, Penn gave them their own assembly, separate from that of Pennsylvania.

Delaware Prospers

Delaware became more prosperous throughout the 1700s. Flour mills, tanneries, and papermaking facilities sprang up along the rivers.

During the French and Indian War, the Three Lower Counties voted to support British General Braddock. They sent cattle and supplies.

In the ten years before the Revolution, people in many colonies complained about being mistreated by the British. The people of Delaware were more content. Many of the taxes were on goods and businesspeople. Most people in Delaware farmed, so taxes did not affect them as much as they did the other colonies. However, they were dependent on other colonies for many goods. Most of them read Philadelphia newspapers, and knew the Pennsylvanians' views.

Working With the Other Colonies

When Massachusetts called a congress of delegates from the colonies in 1765, Delaware joined with the other colonies. The purpose was to present a united plea to the king and Parliament, asking for relief from the high taxes.

Delaware sent two representatives to the Stamp Act Congress. Members of the Congress voted to oppose the Stamp Act and to petition Parliament to repeal it.

Most people in Delaware were happy when the Stamp Act was repealed. They hoped that the problems between England and the colonies were over, but they were just beginning. Parliament then passed the Townshend Acts. The Three Lower Colonies petitioned the king. They declared the Townshend Acts illegal, because the colonies were supposed to have the right to tax themselves.

In 1770, all taxes except for the one on tea were repealed. Delaware appointed a committee of correspondence.

Delaware Demonstrates Against Tax on Tea

When a ship full of tea arrived at Lewes on the Delaware River, eight thousand people kept Captain Ayres from unloading the tea. They let him stay one day to buy supplies, then made him leave the harbor with his cargo.

When news of the closing of the port of Boston reached Delaware, the assembly had an unofficial meeting to elect delegates to the First Continental Congress. A few months later, Delaware had five thousand men ready to fight.

Naval Battle in the Delaware River

During the Revolutionary War, many citizens fled. In March 1776, the heavily armed British warship *Roebuck* started up the Delaware River, followed by the *Liverpool*.

The militia at Wilmington gathered ships and stocked them with guns and ammunition. They opened fire on the English ships when they reached Wilmington. While trying to get closer to the colonists' smaller boats, the *Roebuck* ran aground in the shallow waters. When the tide floated the *Roebuck* off in the morning, both ships sailed back to Lewes.

Sons of the Blue Hen

Captain Jonathan Caldwell's company from Kent County was part of the first Delaware regiment. The men took two gamecocks as mascots. The birds, hatched from eggs of a steel-blue hen, were never beaten in a cockfight. The men rushed into battle, shouting, "We're sons of the Blue Hen, and we're game to the end."[2]

Separating from England

On June 15, 1776, the Delaware assembly voted to sever relations with the British government. Delaware patriot Cesar Rodney had already said in May, "The Continuing to Swear Allegiance to the power that is Cutting our throats . . . is Certainly absurd."[3] He meant it was silly to remain loyal to a country that would not allow them any say in government. When the Second Continental Congress took the vote on declaring independence, both Delaware delegates voted yes.

NORTH CAROLINA

The area that is now North Carolina was first explored in 1524 by Giovanni de Verrazzano. He wrote that the land was "as pleasant and delectable to behold, as is possible to imagine." He spoke of the land's "faire fields and plains."[1]

Lucas Vasquez de Allyon of Spain visited in 1526. He tried to start a colony on the Cape Fear River. When some of their children were taken as slaves, the American Indians wiped out the settlement.

Hernando de Soto went through the area in about 1540 on his search for gold, but was not interested in settling there.

Sir Walter Raleigh

Sir Walter Raleigh, a soldier and explorer, sent two English ships to North Carolina in 1584. The captains claimed all the land along Pamlico Sound for Queen Elizabeth I of England.

They exchanged gifts with the Secotan Indians and set up a trade with them. The Secotan traded furs for tin plates, copper kettles, knives, hatchets, and axes. They also provided food for the men.

When the ships returned to England, they took two of the American Indians, Wanchese and Manteo. The trip had different effects on the two warriors. Manteo became the lifelong friend of the white people, but Wanchese became their deadly enemy.[2]

American Indian Problems

Raleigh sent a number of soldiers in early 1585 to start a colony on Roanoke Island. The leader, Ralph Lane, did not relate well to the American Indians. He torched one village and burned its corn crop because he thought one of the warriors had stolen a silver cup. In another village, he kidnapped the chief's son.

Wanchese and other Secotans planned an attack, but Lane struck first, beheading several of the American Indians. Lane and most of his men went back to England with Sir Francis Drake, an English explorer. They left fifteen men to guard their fort on Roanoke Island.

The Lost Colony

On the next trip, Raleigh wisely chose a more diplomatic leader, Governor John White. The settlers this time included women and children, farmers and tradesmen. They planned to settle further north, but stopped at Roanoke Island to pick up the fifteen men left behind. They found that the fort had been destroyed and no one was there except for a skeleton in one cabin.

The captain refused to go further north, so White and his settlers stayed on Roanoke Island. There, Virginia Dare was the first English child born in North America.

One theory behind the disappearance of the Roanoke colony is that it was wiped out by American Indians who were not on friendly terms with the English settlers.

White went back to England for supplies. When he returned three years later, the houses were destroyed and the colonists were gone. The word "Croatoan" was carved on a tree, so he hoped that they had joined Manteo and the friendly Croatoan people. However, they were never found. Although there are theories about what happened to the "Lost Colony," no one knows for sure.

Scattered Settlements in North Carolina

After that, England lost interest and concentrated on the colony of Virginia. Most of the early North Carolinians were Virginians who drifted south and settled in what is now northeast North Carolina. By 1650, people had settled in the Albemarle region. Some bought land from the American Indians, but others drove them inland.

In 1663 King Charles II gave eight proprietors a charter for the land along the Carolina coast, calling the area simply Carolina, after himself. More settlers came, including craftsmen, laborers, and families.

The Tuscarora War

In 1710, four hundred Swiss settlers settled a large tract of land along the Neuse River. The settlement was called New Bern. In 1711, Tuscarora Indians attacked the village. This was the beginning of the Tuscarora War, which raged for two years. By the war's end, the colonists had killed most of the Tuscarora.

The settlers moved south to found Brunswick Town, on the Cape Fear River. This became North Carolina's most important port. Wealthy planters started large rice plantations along the Cape Fear.

The Early 1700s

In 1712, the Carolina colony was split into North and South Carolina. In 1729, North Carolina became a royal colony when seven of the eight proprietors sold their land to the King. The Scottish governor, Gabriel Johnston, invited his fellow citizens to settle in North Carolina. Many of them settled at Cross Creek, which is now Fayetteville.

In the 1730s, German, Quaker, and Ulster Scot immigrants moved south from Pennsylvania, following the Great Wagon Road through the Shenandoah Valley. In 1752 Moravians, a German religious group, bought one hundred thousand acres of land and started several mission towns. They tried to convert the American Indians to their religion. This conversion effort took place in the area of present-day Winston-Salem.

Most of the American Indians had fled from the area. Large numbers had been killed by the colonists or by disease. The Cherokee remained, living high in the Appalachian Mountains.

Life in North Carolina

North Carolina was divided into two distinct cultures. In the east were farmers, timbermen, merchants, and plantation owners. They lived comfortable lives, and controlled the North Carolina Parliament. Many were English and had financial ties to England.

Life was quite different for the "backcountrymen" in the western part of the colony. Many were German, Quaker, or Scotch-Irish. They had no loyalty to or love for the king. They felt themselves overtaxed, both by England and by the North Carolina Parliament.

War of the Regulation

These feelings led to the War of the Regulation, lasting from 1768 to 1771. The "Regulators" were backcountrymen protesting unfair taxes and repression. They stormed the courthouse in Hillsborough in 1770, and whipped a cheating tax collector named Edmund Fanning. They also attacked the lawyers and ran the judge out of town. Finally, Governor Tryon sent his militia west, where he encountered a crowd of about two thousand Regulators at Great Alamance Creek, near where Burlington is today.

The men asked to speak to the governor. He would not negotiate unless they gave up their arms. They refused and a battle began. After two hours, nine Regulators were dead and many wounded. The militia had similar casualties. Twenty or thirty Regulators were taken prisoner. Later, twelve were tried for treason, and six of those were hung. The other six were pardoned by Tryon.

Discontent with British Policies

In the 1770s, the colonies grew restless and unhappy with British taxation and laws.

Tryon became governor of New York and was replaced by Josiah Martin. When the First Continental Congress was called for September 1774, Martin refused to convene the Assembly to elect delegates.

Some of the leaders called a meeting in Wilmington and elected three delegates. They affirmed their loyalty to the king, but stated their extreme displeasure with Parliament's actions, including the Tea Act. They informed the king that they would not import any British goods except medicine after January 1, 1775, if their concerns were not resolved. They also would stop selling naval stores and tobacco to England.

North Carolina's loyalties were divided. However, by the time of the Declaration of Independence, the colony had sent three delegates to the signing.

12

SOUTH CAROLINA

Almost one hundred years before the English founded the first permanent settlement in South Carolina, the French tried to settle there. Two ships commanded by Jean Ribault landed on the southern coast in 1562. Ribault described the area as "one of the greatest and fayrest havens of the world." He said it had "the best watter of the worlde, and so many sortes of fishes that ye maye take them withowt nett or angle . . . also guinea foule and innumerable wildfoule."[1]

The men set up an outpost there and twenty-seven of them stayed while Ribault went back to France for supplies. He expected to return before the end of the year.

The Colonists Struggle

While he was gone, the men struggled to survive. They ran out of food, so several men sailed to the coast of present-day Georgia and obtained food from American Indians there. Soon after that, their strong house where all the food and supplies were stored burned to the ground. Local American Indians helped rebuild it, but the men were discouraged.

Two settlers drowned when their canoe overturned, and Captain de la Pierria ordered the drummer to be hung for a minor infraction. He also banished another soldier named La Chere to a nearby island as punishment for some unknown offense.

Awaiting Ribault's Return

Meanwhile, Ribault had been held up by a religious war in France. He fought for a while for the Protestants, then gave up on getting help from France. He went to England, and Queen Elizabeth I agreed to help. But before he could return to the New World, he was imprisoned in England as a spy.

An Ill-Fated Voyage

The colonists were low on food and doubted that Ribault would ever return, so they decided to build a ship and return to France. Twenty-one men sailed in the spring of 1563.

Their ship was becalmed (motionless from lack of wind), and they ran out of food. After eating their shoes and other leather items, they resorted to eating one of the men so the rest could live. La Chere was chosen. He was killed and his flesh was eaten. Sources say seven men survived and were eventually rescued from their ship off the English coast.[2]

The First Permanent Settlement

Charles I had granted the area he called "Carolina" to eight Proprietors in 1663. Before that, there were settlers in the Albemarle area of what later became North Carolina as early as 1650.

The first permanent settlement in South Carolina was Charles Town. It was set up by the British on the west bank of the Ashley River when Captain Joseph West brought 148 people. Some of the settlers were from Barbados, where the ship had stopped on the way. Colonel William Sayle had been appointed governor, but he died almost immediately and was replaced by Captain West.

More Settlers Arrive

More settlers from Barbados arrived the next February. Slavery was an important part of life in Barbados, and South Carolina started using slaves almost immediately. Charles Town moved ten miles to Oyster Point in 1680. Several hundred settlers had come from England and the West Indies by then. That same year, a number of Huguenots (French Protestants) arrived.

Africans in South Carolina

Many of those from Barbados were wealthy planters. They captured American Indians and sold them as slaves in the West Indies, then used the money to buy African slaves. The settlers did not like using American Indians as slaves. They were too familiar with the area and could easily escape.[3]

In 1694, Landgrave Thomas Smith successfully grew rice from Madagascar. Then, rice growing really took hold. To cultivate rice, settlers felt they needed more

Enslaved Africans were forced to work in the vast rice fields of South Carolina.

slaves, and the population of Africans in South Carolina grew steadily over the next fifty years.

By 1700, there were thirty-three hundred whites in South Carolina, twenty-four hundred African Americans, and two hundred American Indian slaves.

Ten years later, Africans outnumbered whites forty-three hundred to forty-two hundred. And by 1730, there were twice as many slaves as whites.[4]

South Carolina Becomes Its Own Colony

Some consider 1691 the date when North and South Carolina were separated, because that was the first year a deputy governor was appointed for North Carolina.

However, the proprietor did not actually split the colony until 1712.

American Indians Unite to Drive Out Settlers

During the Tuscarora Indian War, South Carolina spent four thousand British pounds to send an army of settlers and Yamasee Indians to New Bern to help with the fighting. In 1715, the Yamasee turned on them and began attacking European settlements. The Yamasee were eventually joined by fourteen other tribes. The American Indians thought they could wipe out the white settlements and take back the land. Their attempt failed, and in 1717 they gave up. The survivors moved to Florida. However, they continued to attack the settlers in the southern frontiers for many years.

South Carolina Becomes a Royal Colony

In 1719, the colonists were upset because the proprietors had raised the quitrent to four times what it had been. The colonists rose up, forced the proprietors' agent out of office, and elected their own governor. The king decided to make South Carolina a royal colony.

For the first sixty years, most settlement was along the coast. Their ties to England were close. During the 1730s, settlers moved into the interior of the colony. The government provided incentives to landowners who would do so.

Stono Rebellion

Because the slaves far outnumbered the settlers, a slave revolt was possible. In 1739, the Spanish established a camp for runaway slaves near St. Augustine, Florida. On September 9, a number of black people under the leadership of a man named Jemmy attacked a store at Stono's Bridge, near Charles Town (now Charleston). They killed the storekeepers and seized powder and guns.

They marched toward Charles Town, joined by others along the way. The militia assembled. They had more experience with firearms, which made the battle short. About fourteen blacks died in the first volley of shots. Some were captured, then executed. About thirty escaped. A week later, most of the escapees were wiped out thirty miles south on the road to St. Augustine. Twenty whites died in what became known as "Stono's Rebellion."

Cherokee Uprising

The Cherokee were becoming more unhappy with the British colonists. In November 1759, several American Indian chiefs were taken hostage in retaliation for Indian raids. In February 1760, the Cherokee attacked Fort Prince George where the hostages were being held. Twenty-one Cherokee were killed by the soldiers. The Cherokee War ended in 1761. The American Indians signed a treaty with the colonists, opening the way for safe settlement in the interior.

The Bounty Act of 1761 followed. It offered European settlers tax-free land for ten years if they had certificates showing that they were Protestant. Settlers from other colonies poured in, eager for free land.

South Carolinians paid little attention to the Sugar Act in 1764. However, they were upset when they heard about the Stamp Act. The legislature directed Charles Garth, their agent in London, to oppose it.

In 1767, Daniel Moore, a former member of Parliament, was sent to South Carolina to collect taxes. He was met with violent resistance.

The next year, the new governor, Lord Charles Montagu, dissolved the South Carolina House of Commons.

Looking Toward Independence

When the First Continental Congress met in 1774, South Carolina sent five delegates.

South Carolinians donated generously to the suffering citizens of Boston after the harbor was closed. When news came of the Battles of Lexington and Concord, the Provincial Congress of South Carolina raised troops, authorized the printing of paper money to pay for them, and called for the election of a new congress. South Carolina was now involved in the Revolutionary War.

In 1681, King Charles II granted a large area of land to William Penn. The king had owed money to Penn's father, Admiral Sir William Penn. The younger Penn, who had become a Quaker, was satisfied with the land. He had been persecuted for his faith and been imprisoned several times.

PENNSYLVANIA

Penn appointed his cousin, William Markham, governor of the new colony. It included all of New Sweden, plus other land between there and New York. Penn had asked the king to call it New Wales. However, Penn said the Welsh secretary "refused to have it called New Wales, *Sylvania*, and they added *Penn*; and though I much opposed it and went to the king to have it struck out and altered, he said 'twas past."[1]

Penn made up a plan called the *First Frame of Government* for the new colony. It included much of his philosophy of government. He wrote ". . . as governments are made and moved by men, so by them they are ruined, too. . . . Let men be good, and the government cannot be bad; if it is ill, they will cure it."[2]

William Penn Arrives

Penn arrived in Pennsylvania in 1682. He met with the Delaware Indians and paid them for their land, although they did not really understand that people could own land. His relations with them were always friendly, because he treated them well.

Penn met with the new Pennsylvania Assembly, and they approved the *Frame*. They also set up a code of law called the *Great Law*.

At the next assembly, in March 1683, the members asked for some changes in the *Frame*. He asked if they would prefer a new charter, and they agreed. On April 2, the *Second Frame of Government* was adopted. The main change was to limit the power of the governor.

William Penn (standing with arms open) negotiated a treaty with the local American Indians.

Early Explorers

Penn's settlement was not the first in Pennsylvania. In 1608, Henry Hudson had sailed up the Delaware River, searching for a passage through North America. European countries wanted to find a shortcut to the Far East, where they could get spices.

Frenchman Etienne Brule was the first white man known to have reached the interior of Pennsylvania. He sailed from northern New York down the Susquehanna River through Pennsylvania and Maryland in 1615.

The Dutch built Fort Nassau across the Delaware River from the spot where Philadelphia was later built. They were interested in trade rather than settlement.

The first settlers in Pennsylvania were a group of Swedes and Finns under Peter Minuit. The group arrived in 1638 and built Fort Christina. Minuit bought the land from the American Indians.

Then, he set off for Sweden to get more settlers and supplies. His ship was lost at sea, and he was never seen again. The men left behind managed to survive, with the help of the friendly Delaware. In 1640, Peter Hollender arrived with another shipload of colonists and supplies, and a third ship brought more settlers that fall.

The Swedes cut down trees and built cabins, as they had done at home. They were the first to build log cabins in the New World.

New Sweden

In 1643, Johan Printz became governor of New Sweden, as the area was called. He ruled for ten years. He was replaced by Johann Classon Rising. Rising seized the Dutch Fort Casimir on the Delaware River.

Peter Stuyvesant, governor of New Netherland, retaliated. He took an army of three hundred soldiers, as well as seven ships, and sailed to the Delaware. He not only recaptured Fort Casimir, but he also forced the Swedes to surrender all of New Sweden. It now became part of New Netherland. However, the settlers in New Sweden were treated well, and few of them went back to Sweden.

The Dutch reign in New Sweden lasted about ten years. Then, Sir Robert Carr, an English captain, seized the area for the English. New Amsterdam became New York. England controlled the area after that, except for a brief period in 1673 when the Dutch recaptured New Amsterdam and the Delaware country. A treaty returned the land to the English in 1674. Edmund Andros was named governor and the English system of laws and justice went into effect.

In 1683, Francis Daniel Pastorius and a group of German settlers founded Germantown. It was just outside Philadelphia.

In August 1684, problems arose with Lord Baltimore in Maryland. He and Penn claimed some of the same land. Penn returned to England to try to straighten it out. While he was there, King Charles II died. He was succeeded by James II, also a friend of Penn's.

James was not in power long. The "Glorious Revolution" of 1688 drove him from the throne. He was replaced by William and Mary, who did not trust Penn.

They thought the proprietor had been too close to Charles and James Stuart.

King William relieved Penn of his governorship in 1692 when he created the Dominion of New England, but in 1694 Penn was restored as governor.

While Penn was in England, Quakers in Germantown staged a protest against slavery, the first in the New World. It had little effect on slavery in the colonies, but most of the Germans did not use slaves.

Penn finally returned in 1699. Some of the leaders in the Assembly asked for the frame of government to be rewritten in a more democratic way. In 1701, Penn and the Assembly agreed on the *Charter of Privileges*, which

SOURCE DOCUMENT

KNOW YE THEREFORE, THAT FOR THE FURTHER WELL-BEING AND GOOD GOVERNMENT OF THE SAID PROVINCE, AND TERRITORIES; AND IN PURSUANCE OF THE RIGHTS AND POWERS BEFORE-MENTIONED, I THE SAID WILLIAM PENN DO DECLARE, GRANT AND CONFIRM, UNTO ALL THE FREEMEN, PLANTERS AND ADVENTURERS, AND OTHER INHABITANTS OF THIS PROVINCE AND TERRITORIES, THESE FOLLOWING LIBERTIES, FRANCHISES AND PRIVILEGES, SO FAR AS IN ME LIETH, TO BE HELD, ENJOYED AND KEPT, BY THE FREEMEN, PLANTERS AND ADVENTURERS, AND OTHER INHABITANTS OF AND IN THE SAID PROVINCE AND TERRITORIES "HEREUNTO ANNEXED, FOR EVER.[3]

The Charter of Privileges endured as the basis of Pennsylvania's government for almost seventy-five years.

continued as the plan of government until the American Revolution. The Pennsylvania Constitution was based on it when Pennsylvania became a state.

Then, Penn returned to England, never to see Pennsylvania again. However, he always took great interest in the colony, right up to his death in 1718.

Pennsylvania had an important leader in Benjamin Franklin, who had been born in Boston and moved to Philadelphia as a young boy. After working in a print shop in England for a while, he returned to Philadelphia and managed a print shop. Later, he set up his own shop. Franklin published a newspaper, served as postmaster of Philadelphia, and invented many useful items.

Things went well in Pennsylvania until 1753, when there was trouble with the French and the American Indians. The French built Fort Presque Isle on Lake Erie and Fort Le Boeuf a few miles from there. The governor of Virginia sent George Washington, a young soldier from Virginia, to Fort Le Boeuf. He then politely

Benjamin Franklin was a printer and inventor. He also became an important American patriot and attended the Constitutional Convention in 1787.

informed the French that they were trespassing on English territory. His visit had no effect.

The English built a fort at the Forks of the Ohio, where Pittsburgh now stands. The French captured the fort and called it Fort Duquesne. In 1755, British General Braddock, with Washington second in command, attacked the fort. It was a bloody battle and the British lost about half their men, including Braddock himself.

Three years later, the British recaptured Fort Duquesne. They named it Fort Pitt, for William Pitt, British prime minister. In 1759, the British captured Fort Niagara. The fighting ended the next year.

The Treaty of Paris of 1763 awarded all of North America to England, except for New Orleans. That was given to Spain. But the Indian problems were far from over. Chief Pontiac had a vision. He told his tribe that he spoke with the Great Spirit, who told him:

> I am the Maker of heaven and earth . . . . The land on which you live I have made for you, and not for others. . . . And as for these English—these dogs, dressed in red, who have come to rob you of your hunting-grounds, and drive away the game—you must lift the hatchet against them. Wipe them from the face of the earth, and then you will have my favor back again, and once more be happy and prosperous.[4]

Pontiac got many tribes together to try to drive the English out. They began attacking English forts in 1763. Colonel Henry Bouquet finally stopped the attackers at a battle in Bushy Run in Westmoreland County. This was the most important American Indian battle fought in

Pennsylvania. The American Indians asked for peace, and a treaty was negotiated.

American Indian troubles were over, but troubles with the British government were just beginning. In 1765, Philadelphia merchants protested the Stamp Act. Three years later, the colony adopted the nonimportation resolutions, agreeing not to import goods from England.

The First Continental Congress met in Carpenter's Hall in Philadelphia in 1774. The next year, the Second Continental Congress met at the State House, now Independence Hall. Benjamin Franklin was one of the delegates from Pennsylvania.

The Declaration of Independence was approved in July 1776 and signed the next month. Pennsylvania played a big part in the events leading up to the Revolution.

GEORGIA

Europeans first visited Georgia in the year 1539. Hernando de Soto led a group searching for gold. Although the American Indians gave them shelter along the way, they destroyed a village where Rome, Georgia, now stands. They took some American Indians hostage and made others slaves, and took all the grain the Indians had stored for winter.

In 1566, Spanish priests started missions on Jekyll Island and St. Simons Island. South Carolinians saw the nearby missions as a threat to their land. By 1686, the Spanish had retreated south of the St. Mary's River, now the boundary between Georgia and Florida.

James Oglethorpe's Part in Settling Georgia

By the early 1700s, most of the east coast had been settled by Europeans. England claimed Georgia. James Oglethorpe, a former member of the House of Commons (part of the legislature of England), wanted to help the poor, especially those in prison.

People who could not pay their debts, or money owed, were often imprisoned. Oglethorpe objected and worked to ensure better treatment for those in debtors' prison. Partly because of his committee's investigations,

Parliament released ten thousand prisoners in 1730. Most of them were debtors.

Oglethorpe's friend, Dr. Thomas Bray, a leading philanthropist (one who spends money to help others), suggested setting up a colony for debtors. When Bray died, Oglethorpe took up his idea. He obtained a charter on January 27, 1732, granting him all the territory between the Savannah and Aoltamaha rivers and westward to the Pacific. According to the royal charter, this land had belonged to South Carolina, but now became "one Independent and separate Province by the name of Georgia."[1]

Twenty-three trustees, including Oglethorpe, would rule the colony for twenty-one years, then the king would decide on Georgia's form of government. A trustee could not own land, hold office, or receive pay for his work for the new colony.

Most Settlers Not Prisoners

It is often said that Georgia was settled by prisoners. That is not entirely true, however. According to historian Albert B. Saye, no more than a dozen of the settlers had been in debtors prison.[2] Instead, Oglethorpe sought poor people. Possibly many would have gone to debtors prison if they had stayed in England.

The trustees paid the settlers' way to Georgia. The shipload of settlers sailed for its destination from England on November 17, 1732.

Oglethorpe's Voyage

Oglethorpe proved himself a leader on the trip across the Atlantic. He provided for the needs of the people, sometimes out of his private stores. He settled arguments and caught a dolphin to provide meat for pregnant women, who needed it more than the others.

Land was sighted on January 13, 1733, but it was South Carolina. The colony's governor would not let Oglethorpe's group land, for fear they might decide to settle there. Oglethorpe went ashore and gave Governor Johnson and his Council a copy of the Georgia charter, asking their advice. They were so impressed with him that the Carolina Assembly provided one hundred head of cattle, five bulls, twenty sows, four boars, and twenty barrels of rice to the new colony, as well as several boats.

Oglethorpe's Settlement

On February 1, the group arrived at Uamacraw Bluff. This was the site Oglethorpe had chosen for their settlement. It was here that the city of Savannah started.

James Oglethorpe went to great lengths to protect the colonists in Georgia.

Everyone went to work unloading boats and moving goods to the town site. They cut down trees and built a fort. Some cleared land for planting. Oglethorpe supervised it all. The town was laid out in a pattern still recognizable in present-day Savannah.

Houses were built, crops were planted, and the palisade completed. Along with a guardhouse and two blockhouses, it would protect the town against attack.

The Georgians ate food from their gardens, but South Carolina and the American Indians also provided needed food. Oglethorpe had done a good job of gaining the friendship and help of the American Indians.

Hard Times in Georgia

There were a number of deaths in 1733, the colony's first year. Many thought it was due to the climate and lack of a pure water supply, but Oglethorpe blamed the deaths on the consumption of rum. On July 11, when sixty people in Savannah were ill, a ship brought forty-two Jews from England. They were not expected, but were welcomed. Dr. Nunis went to work as soon as he got off the ship and saved the lives of the ill.

The settlers came from a variety of places and backgrounds. All religions except Catholics were welcomed. Oglethorpe could not understand the dissatisfaction of the people. They were unhappy with the land system, under which wives and daughters could not inherit land. Many wanted to own slaves and were unhappy because some would not work and others were unable to. They also did not like Oglethorpe's insistence on no rum.

Conflict Between English and Spanish

There were also problems between the English in Georgia and the Spanish in Florida. Oglethorpe made a trip to England in 1736 to raise money for the colony, and to raise an armed force to help in an anticipated conflict with Spain. He was given a regiment of seven hundred men.

In September 1738, Oglethorpe returned to Georgia with his regiment. They were headquartered at Fort Fredrica on St. Simons Island. The next September, a ship from Rhode Island brought an incorrect message that England had declared war on Spain. Oglethorpe's militia got ready for battle. He recruited a thousand American Indian warriors to help.

In mid-November, the Spanish attacked Amelia Island and killed two men. Oglethorpe's men headed for the St. Johns River, destroying Spanish boats along the way. They then battled with Spanish troops on the river.

They regrouped at Frederica, then started south on December 1, taking several cannons and many American Indians. They captured the Spanish Fort San Francisco de Pupa, which controlled traffic on the St. Johns River. Communications between St. Augustine and the area to the west were cut off.

The War of Jenkins's Ear

This came to be known as the War of Jenkins's Ear. It was called that because Robert Jenkins, captain of an English ship, claimed that Spanish guards had cut off his ear in

1731. He showed the ear to British Parliament, turning public opinion against the Spanish.

Much of the war was fought in Georgia and Florida. In 1741, the Spanish attacked Cumberland Island, off the coast of Georgia. Then the main Spanish fleet appeared off the coast of St. Simons Island. Just as the Spanish reached the marshes on the island, it began to rain.

Oglethorpe's troops piled up logs and brush to build barricades. When the Spanish soldiers went around the makeshift barricades, the English bombarded the Spaniards with musket fire.

When Oglethorpe returned with more troops, his men had held off the Spanish for nearly an hour. The Spanish finally retreated, because they could not tell how many English soldiers were hiding in the woods and behind the barricades. The water in the marsh was supposedly red with the blood of the soldiers, so it was called the Battle of Bloody Marsh. This was the last time the Spanish attacked Georgia.

Changes in Georgia's Economy

At the end of the war, Oglethorpe returned to England permanently. Georgia had not done well financially under the trustee system. It was not until 1749 that the colonists exported the first goods.

The next year, slavery was permitted. By 1773, there were almost as many slaves as whites. There were fifteen thousand slaves and eighteen thousand whites.[3]

In 1752, Georgia became a royal colony. The major products were naval stores (products from pine trees), lumber, and indigo. Farmers grew rice along the coast, although the average farmer could not afford to build the dikes needed to grow it. Inland, they grew wheat and other grains.

Georgia Under Royal Governors

John Reynolds, the first royal governor, was unpopular because he tried to move the capital from Savannah to Hardwicke, in the south. Henry Ellis replaced him, but did not last long because he did not like the heat. Under the third and last royal governor, James Wright, the colony's economy greatly improved.

The trustees had wanted the colonists to produce silk, and had decreed that anyone receiving land grants must plant two mulberry trees per acre as food for silkworms.[4] Early attempts at producing silk were unsuccessful, but between 1760 and 1775, about one thousand pounds of raw silk were exported annually.[5]

Georgians More Content

By the 1770s, when Virginia and the northern colonies were grumbling about oppression by the British, most Georgians were content. Exports were at an all-time high and an abundance of crops grew in the rich soil. Slavery contributed to the prosperity.

As in the other colonies, the Georgians' loyalties were divided between the king and America. However, enough Georgians opposed the King for them to join the other twelve colonies when they declared independence in 1776.

FROM DECLARATION TO CONSTITUTION

Although the colonies declared their independence in 1776, there were many problems to be solved before the new country would run smoothly. The first was winning the war.

Two Armies

The British dominated the early part of the war. They had a well-trained army and a large navy. Their military structure had been in place for many years. The Americans, on the other hand, were still struggling to build an army and navy and to set up a government.

The Americans had the advantage of fighting on their own ground, so they did not have to bring in military forces and supplies from abroad. They were more committed to the war, since it directly affected them. Starting in 1777, the Americans had help from Europe, especially from the French.

Fighting in New England

The first part of the war was fought in New England, starting in 1775 when the British sent troops to put down rebellion in Boston. In March 1776, the British evacuated Boston, because they had decided it was not a good place for their headquarters. It was hard to defend, and most of the radical patriots were there. However, they realized that the colonies were unified in this attempt to gain independence. Therefore, they could not concentrate all their efforts in one area.

War Comes to the Middle Atlantic States

The second phase of the war was fought in the Mid-Atlantic Region. Here, the British came dangerously close to crushing the rebellion. The colonists were becoming discouraged because of the great odds they faced.

On Christmas Day 1776, George Washington's officers read Thomas Paine's new pamphlet—*The American Crisis I,* which came to be known as *Common Sense*—aloud to their troops.[1] The pamphlet began: "These are the times that try men's souls. The summer soldier and the sunshine patriot will, in this crisis, shrink from the service of their country. . . . Tyranny, like hell, is not easily conquered."[2]

Inspired, the troops crossed the Delaware River and launched a surprise attack on the British troops at Trenton. Most were hired German soldiers, known as Hessians. Washington knew the Germans made a great celebration of Christmas, and expected the soldiers to be tired after a day of celebrating.

It was a brilliant idea. Washington took the British and Hessians completely by surprise. The Americans captured a thousand prisoners and most of the enemy's stores, including many German swords. This victory gave the Americans new determination.

British Plan Fails

The British had a plan to cut the United States into two parts by taking New York State. General Howe would march up the Hudson River from New York to Albany. General John Burgoyne was to march down from Canada to Albany, capturing Fort Ticonderoga and other forts along the way. General Barry St. Leger would march east from Canada along the Mohawk River. All would meet at Albany in October 1777.

At the last minute, Howe decided to attack Philadelphia instead. The campaign in New York failed, and Burgoyne's forces were solidly defeated at Saratoga, a great victory and turning point for the Americans.

After the Turning Point

A few months later, France recognized the new country and furnished money and military assistance, including the use of its navy. The navy played an important part in the final phase of the war.

The last years of the revolution, from 1778 on, took place in the South. Britain had some important military victories during this time. They captured Savannah, Georgia, and Charleston, South Carolina, both important seaports.

Washington decided to try to trap British general Lord Cornwallis on the peninsula at Yorktown, Virginia. With the help of the French fleet, he was successful.

When Cornwallis surrendered, the fighting was over except for a few small skirmishes.

The Treaty of Paris

The Treaty of Paris was finally signed on September 3, 1783. It recognized the United States and gave it the territory from the southern boundary of Canada to the northern boundary of Florida. Its land extended westward from the Atlantic Ocean to the Mississippi River.

Articles of Confederation Adopted

While the fighting was going on, the Americans found it necessary to put some sort of government in place. A document called the Articles of Confederation was written and submitted to the Congress just eight days after the signing of the Declaration of Independence.

The states were given as much independence as possible. However, it took several years before all the states approved the articles. They disagreed on boundary lines and conflicting decisions of courts in different states. They did not agree on the number of representatives and votes each state should have in Congress. The document was finally ratified (approved) by all the states in 1781.

Problems with the Articles of Confederation

After the war, Americans realized that the Articles of Confederation were not going to work. The federal government had very little power. Any measures passed by Congress had to be approved by nine of the thirteen states.

Congress could not raise money by collecting taxes. It also did not have control over foreign trade.

The Constitutional Convention

By the late 1780s, most Americans were unhappy with the government. In 1787, fifty-five men from all the states except Rhode Island, met in Philadelphia to make changes to the Articles of Confederation so that Congress could effectively govern the country.

Coming to an Agreement

Most of the delegates agreed that the United States needed a stronger government, but there was disagreement on how strong it should be. However, after weeks of arguments, the delegates compromised. They created a committee to settle the differences and decided that an entirely new Constitution was needed.

Two Different Documents

James Madison drafted most of the new Constitution. It differed from the Articles of Confederation in several ways. Congress consisted of one house under the Articles. The new constitution provided for two houses, the Senate and the House of Representatives. Each state would have two senators. The number of representatives would depend on the population of the state.

Members of Congress would be elected by the people. Before, they had been appointed by the state legislatures. There would be a separate judicial branch of government. It would consist of the Supreme Court and

---

SOURCE DOCUMENT

WE, THE PEOPLE OF THE UNITED STATES, IN ORDER TO FORM A MORE PERFECT UNION, ESTABLISH JUSTICE, INSURE DOMESTIC TRANQUILITY, PROVIDE FOR THE COMMON DEFENSE, PROMOTE THE GENERAL WELFARE, AND SECURE THE BLESSINGS OF LIBERTY TO OURSELVES AND OUR POSTERITY, DO ORDAIN AND ESTABLISH THIS CONSTITUTION FOR THE UNITED STATES OF AMERICA.[3]

The Constitution has survived over two hundred years and remains the basis of the United States government today. The above excerpt is from the Preamble of the Constitution.

other courts. There would be an executive branch, headed by a president.

The Constitution Is Ratified

Of course, everyone was not satisfied with the new Constitution. A Bill of Rights, which became the first ten amendments to the Constitution, was added. In June 1788, the ninth state ratified the Constitution, putting it into effect. The other four states ratified it after that.

In 1789, George Washington was easily elected the first president of the United States. For the first time, the states were united under a strong leader the people had elected themselves. The first thirteen states had come a long way from their humble beginning as thirteen separate colonies, each battling for its own survival. Now they were part of a nation that had gained the world's respect and looked to a prosperous future.

★ TIMELINE ★

1587—The lost colony is founded at Roanoke, in present-day North Carolina.

1607—Jamestown, Virginia, becomes first permanent settlement in the colonies.

1612—The first tobacco is planted in Virginia.

1619—The House of Burgesses in Virginia is first elected assembly in New World; the first slaves in the New World arrive in Virginia.

1620—Pilgrims settle at Plymouth, Massachusetts.

1623—David Thompson starts the first settlement in New Hampshire.

1624—The Dutch buy Manhattan from American Indians and start a settlement in New York.

1630—The Massachusetts Bay Colony is founded; Swedes settle Pavonia in New Jersey.

1634—Colonists sent by Lord Baltimore settle in Maryland.

1636—Rhode Island is founded by Roger Williams; Thomas Hooker founds Connecticut.

1638—The first permanent settlement in Delaware is started.

1663—The Carolinas are chartered.

1664—England takes over New Netherland from the Dutch.

1675—King Phillip's War begins.

1676—Bacon's Rebellion takes place.

1682—William Penn founds Pennsylvania.

1685—The northern colonies are combined into one large colony called New England.

1692—The Salem witchcraft trials take place.

1712—North and South Carolina become separate colonies.

1733—James Oglethorpe founds Georgia.

1754—The French and Indian War is fought.
-1763

1763—The Treaty of Paris gives land in North America to England; the Mason-Dixon line is drawn by surveyors.

1764—The Sugar Act is passed.

1765—The Stamp Act is passed.

1768—The War of the Regulation is fought.
-1771

1770—The Boston Massacre occurs.

1773—The Boston Tea Party takes place.

1774—The Intolerable Acts are passed.

1775—The Battles of Lexington and Concord are fought.

1776—The Declaration of Independence is signed.

★ CHAPTER NOTES ★

Chapter 1. The Colonies Declare Independence

1. The Trustees of Indiana University, "The Declaration of Independence of the Thirteen Colonies," *Indiana University School of Law—Bloomington*, © 2001 <http://www.law.indiana.edu/uslawdocs/declaration.html> (September 18, 2003).

2. "Signing the Declaration of Independence," *Ben's Guide to U.S. Government*, May 8, 2000, <http://bensguide.gpo.gov/6-8/documents/declaration/signers.html> (August 13, 2003).

Chapter 2. Virginia

1. "Jamestown," © 1994–2000, <www.williamsburg.com/james/james.html> (August 13, 2003).

2. Louis D. Rubin, Jr., *Virginia: A Bicentennial History* (NY: Norton, 1977), p. 3.

3. Ibid., p. 5.

4. "John Smith Describes the 'Starving Time' at Jamestown, 1609–1610," *American Passages*, © 2002 <http://www.wadsworth.com/history_d/special_features/ext/ap/chapter2/2.2.JohnSmith.html> (October 8, 2003)

5. Rubin, p. 9.

6. "The Fairfax Resolves, July 6–18, 1774," *George Washington Papers*, <http://memory.loc.gov/ammem/gwthml/gwfairfax.html> (September 29, 2003).

7. "Give Me Liberty Or Give Me Death," *The American Revolution*, n.d., <http://theamericanrevolution.org/ipeople/phenry/phenryspeech.asp> (October 8, 2003).

Chapter 3. Massachusetts

1. Dale Taylor, *The Writer's Guide to Everyday Life in Colonial America From 1607–1783* (Cincinnati: Writer's Digest Books, 1997), p. 6.

2. "Mayflower Compact 1620," *The Lillian Goldman Law Library in Memory of Sol Goldman*, 1996–2003, <http://www.yale.edu/lawweb/avalon/amerdoc/mayflower.htm> (September 18, 2003).

3. John Harris, *Saga of the Pilgrims from Europe to the New World* (Chester, Conn.: Globe Pequot Press, 1990), p. 85.

4. Taylor, p. 8.

5. William Bradford, *Bradford's History of Plymouth Plantation*, ed. William T. Davis (New York: W. W. Norton & Co., 1908), p. 299.

6. James Deetz and Patricia Scott Deetz, *The Times of Their Lives: Life, Love, and Death in Plymouth Colony* (New York: W. H. Freeman, 2000), p. 89.

7. Ronald W. McGranahan, "Lexington and Concord," The American Revolution Home Page, © 1998–2002, <http://www.americanrevwar.homestead.com/files/LEXCOM.htm> (August 13, 2003).

Chapter 4. New Hampshire

1. "A Brief History of New Hampshire," *The NH Almanac*, n.d. <http://www.state.nh/nhinfo/history.html> (August 13, 2003).

2. Elizabeth Forbes Morison and Elting E. Morison, *New Hampshire: A Bicentennial History* (New York: W. W. Norton & Company, 1976), p. 13.

Chapter 5. New York

1. "Giovanni da Verrazzano's Report to Francis I, July 8, 1524," *Long Island Our Story*, n.d., <http://www.newsday.com/extras/lihistory/vault/hs215alv.htm> (August 13, 2003).

2. Michael Kammen, *Colonial New York: A History* (New York: Charles Scribner's Sons, 1975), p. 1.

3. "The New Netherland Colony," *A Brief Outline of Dutch History and the Province of New Netherland*, n.d., <http://www.coins.nd.edu/ColCoin/ColCoinIntros/Netherlands.html> (August 13, 2003).

4. Kammen, p. 71.

5. "The Articles of Association; October 20, 1774," *The Avalon Project at Yale Law School*, © 1999, <http://www.yale.edu/lawweb/avalon/contcong/10-20-74.htm> (September 18, 2003).

Chapter 6. New Jersey

1. "Full Text of Robert Juet's Journal," *Long Island Our Story*, n.d., <http://www.newsday.com/extras/lihistory/vault/hs216alv.htm> (August 13, 2003).

2. "Part V: And that the Planting of the Said Province," *The Concessions and Agreements of the Proprietors of East Jersey*,

© 1996–2003 <http://www.nj.gov/njfacts/concess5.htm> (September 18, 2003).

Chapter 7. Maryland

1. Matthew Page Andrews, *History of Maryland: Province and State* (Garden City, N.Y.: Doubleday, Doran & Company, Inc., 1929), p. 13.

2. "The Colony of Maryland," <http://colonialancestors.com/md/md23.htm> (September 12, 2003).

3. Andrews, p. 19.

Chapter 8. Connecticut

1. "Connecticut History," <http://www.kids.state.ct.us/history.htm> (September 12, 2003).

Chapter 9. Rhode Island

1. Carleton Beals, *Colonial Rhode Island* (Camden, N.J.: T. Nelson, 1970), p. 9

2. Ibid., p. 31.

3. "Providence Agreement," *Documents of Colonial American History*, n.d., <www.jate.u=szeged.hu/~gnovak/s99f32RI1637.htm> (September 29, 2003).

4. Beals, p. 55.

5. "Narragansett History," July 26, 2003, <http://www.dickshovel.com/Narra.html> (August 13, 2003).

Chapter 10. Delaware

1. Gardell Dano Christensen and Eugenia Burney, *Colonial Delaware* (Nashville: T. Nelson, 1974), pp. 20–21.

2. Ibid., p. 120.

3. John A. Munroe, *Colonial Delaware: A History* (Millwood, N.Y.: KTO Press, 1978), p. 252.

Chapter 11. North Carolina

1. Sheila Turnage, *North Carolina* (Oakland, Calif.: Compass America Guides, 2002), p. 20.

2. Ibid., p. 21.

Chapter 12. South Carolina

1. Robert M. Weir, *Colonial South Carolina: A History* (Columbia: University of South Carolina Press, 1993), p. 33.

2. "Charlesfort: History of the French Settlement," n.d., <http://www.cla.sc.edu/sciaa/staff/depratterc/chas1.html> (August 13, 2003).

3. Francis Jennings, *The Creation of America: Through Revolution to Empire* (New York: Cambridge University Press, 2000), p. 44.

4. Ibid.

Chapter 13. Pennsylvania

1. Sylvester K. Stevens, *Pennsylvania: Birthplace of a Nation* (New York: Random House, 1964), p. 31.

2. Ibid., p. 33.

3. "Charter of Privileges Granted by William Penn, esq. to the Inhabitants of Pennsylvania and Territories, October 28, 1701," *The Avalon Project at Yale Law School*, © 1998 <http://www.yale.edu/lawweb/avalon/states/pa07.htm> (September 18, 2003).

4. Joseph J. Kelley, Jr., *Pennsylvania, The Colonial Years: 1681–1776* (Garden City, N.Y.: Doubleday and Company, Inc., 1980), p. 463.

Chapter 14. Georgia

1. Kenneth Coleman, *Colonial Georgia* (New York: Charles Scribner's Sons, 1976), p. 17.

2. Albert B. Saye, *New Viewpoints in Georgia History* (Athens: University of Georgia Press, 1943), p. v.

3. John T. Edge, *Georgia* (Oakland, Calif.: Compass American Guides, 2002), p. 19.

4. Ibid., p. 17.

5. Coleman, p. 209.

Chapter 15. From Declaration to Constitution

1. Jack Fruchtman, Jr., *Thomas Paine: Apostle of Freedom* (New York: Four Walls Eight Windows, 1994), p. 94.

2. Thomas Paine, "The American Crisis," n.d., <http://libertyonline.hypermall.com/Paine/Crisis/Crisis-TOC.html> (August 13, 2003).

3. Cornell Law School, "The Constitution of the United States of America," *The Legal Information Institute*, n.d., <http://www.law.cornell.edu/constitution/constitution.preamble.html> (September 18, 2003).

★ Further Reading ★

Books

Burgan, Michael. *Colonial and Revolutionary Times*. New York: Franklin Watts, 2003.

Collier, Christopher. *The French and Indian War*. Tarrytown, N.Y.: Benchmark Books, 1998.

Egger-Bovet, Howard. *USKids History*. Boston: Little, Brown, 1996.

Hakim, Joy. *From Colonies to Country*. New York: Oxford University Press, 2003.

Kent, Zachary. *The Mysterious Disappearance of Roanoke Colony in American History*. Berkeley Heights, N.J.: Enslow Publishers, Inc., 2004.

McGowen, Tom. *The Revolutionary War and George Washington's Army in American History*. Berkeley Heights, N.J.: Enslow Publishers, Inc., 2004.

Nobleman, Marc Tyler. *The Thirteen Colonies*. Minneapolis: Compass Point Books, 2002.

Steins, Richard. *Colonial America*. Austin, Tex.: Raintree Steck-Vaughn, 2000.

Internet Addresses

"Ratifying the Constitution." *Congress for Kids*. n.d. <http://www.congressforkids.net/Constitution_ratifyingconstitution.htm>.

Cybrarian Kids' Educational Curriculum Site. "Colonization." *Early America*. 1997–2001. <http://www.cybrary.org/colonial.htm>.

The National Park Service ParkNet. "Children in Colonial Times." *Fort Frederica*. n.d. <http://www.nps.gov/fofr/col_kids.htm>.

★ INDEX ★